THE PYRAMID PRINCIPLE

**A BATTLE-TESTED
HALL-OF-FAMER DISCOVERS
UCLA COACH JOHN WOODEN'S
TRUE MEANING OF SUCCESS**

BASED ON THE TRUE STORY OF
JOHN VALLELY WITH PAUL WEISSENSTEIN

The Pyramid Principle

A Battle-Tested Hall-of-Famer Discovers
UCLA Coach John Wooden's True Meaning of Success
Based on the True Story of John Vallely with Paul Weissenstein

2024 © by John Vallely with Paul Weissenstein

Printed in the United States of America

Spirit Media and our logos are trademarks of Spirit Media

꩜ **SpiritMedia.US**
www.spiritmedia.us
8045 Arco Corporate Dr STE 130
Raleigh, NC 27617
1 (888) 800-3744

Books › Self Help › Personal Transformation
Books › Biographies › Sports Biographies

Paperback ISBN: 979-8-89307-115-3
Hardback ISBN: 979-8-89307-116-0
Audiobook ISBN: 979-8-89307-118-4
eBook ISBN: 979-8-89307-117-7
Library of Congress Control Number: 2024918727

DEDICATION

My son Eric is a powerful force of courage and commitment and was a cornerstone of stability when it felt like my world was falling apart.

When his nine-year-old younger sister was diagnosed with cancer, Eric became a special teammate and champion of hers. It was hard for me to even see straight after we lost Erin at age twelve, but Eric remained steadfast and kept me grounded by saying, "Dad, we are still a family."

Eric would go off to school at UCLA, play on two NCAA championship volleyball teams, graduate on time, and start his adult life. He has always been the special glue that helps keep us together. He married his wife Suzanne, and they have our talented granddaughter Vivian, who attends Pepperdine University and competes on the swim and dive team.

It is with great joy that Karen and I honor and dedicate our family story to our son, Eric Vallely.

INTRODUCTION

In Houston's MD Anderson's Cancer Center, one pint of stem cells, flown in directly from Germany, passed drip by drip into my bloodstream. Far from my NBA days as a former first-rounder and a Houston Rocket, my best shot at survival hung in that bag. I was starting from scratch. My blood count registered at zero: no red cells, no white cells, just stem cells. Even in my nervous state, I could tell something was wrong. Sure enough, the central venous catheter line that was transporting the stem cells to my system had ruptured, and blood was spilling out and pooling on the floor.

My daughter's questions from years before had unexpectedly become mine: "Daddy, will I survive a transplant?" followed by "Will I live to see Christmas?" Amid a life journey that has placed me among UCLA Hall of Famers, locked me in a courtroom battle with the Bank of America, and inflicted my darling daughter Erin with cancer, suddenly I was in my fight to stay alive in a rematch with Non-Hodgkin's Lymphoma.

In that moment of despair, I needed to find a way to hold on to hope in the face of uncertainty. As I wrestled to find God's strength for my weakness in this battle, my only recourse was to turn to the same source of guidance and wisdom I have used for every critical struggle in my own life: the words and teachings of John Wooden, my UCLA basketball coach and a man I consider the greatest teacher of his time.

TABLE OF CONTENTS

Chapter 1
THE JOURNEY BEGINS

"Even my own mom said I was too slow."

~ **John Vallely**

This incredible journey all started with a dream, a ball, and the sweet sound of a one-dribble pull-up and a basketball swishing through a hoop. It is a sound that is so pure, so soothing, a satisfying reward for executing the perfect shot: no rim, no backboard, nothing but net. The ultimate dream would be executing the ideal shot for the legendary Coach John Wooden and the Blue and Gold of UCLA.

In 1935, my father bought a bayfront property for $7,000 in the Southern California town of Newport Beach. He built bedrooms for me and my sister then hung a backboard up on the garage. Initially, my family complained about the constant sound of the ball bouncing off the basket. After years of dedication, my shot was so smooth that the noise could only be described as calming. Even my dribbling sounded rhythmic. Whether it was on the alleyway asphalt or the hardwood floor, that sound would change my life and one day lead to hope. During those years, I would spend hours upon hours in the alley shooting baskets, intoxicated by the sound and relentless in my efforts to hear it again and again.

The other sound that defined my childhood was the splash of waves hitting a moving sailboat.

Balboa Island, a harborside community in Newport Harbor, is one of the largest recreational boat and yacht harbors in the United States and the home of the most beautiful sunsets in the world. Sometimes referred to as the "Southern California Riviera," it was a magical place to grow up. Even Hollywood film stars like John Wayne and Shirley Temple came to gain summer inspiration on the bayfront, along with industry tycoons who docked their yachts at their seaside mansions. Relaxed and charming to this day, it feels like a return to 1950 on Marine Avenue.

Accessible to the public via bridge or ferry, the Fun Zone Arcade quickly became a destination for kids from all over Orange County. They would come to hang out, play skee ball, ride the Ferris Wheel, eat ice cream, or take a midnight swim beneath the glow of the 1,500 pavilion light bulbs that cast a glimmer on the water. It was a perfect island for vacationers. Many came for boat tours in hopes of seeing blue or orca whales jumping from the crystal-clear water. Some rented boats to travel or fish for mackerel beyond the Balboa Pier. Others would rent paddle boards, canoes, and sailboats to explore or float and dream as the colors faded at sunset on the Newport Beach horizon, from red to orange to purple. Countless came for the white sand beaches. For some, it was just a place to eat the best corn dogs, frozen bananas, and saltwater taffy on the west coast.

It was a great location for my father's business, Vallely Boat Rental. For as long as I can remember, he owned and operated this enterprise where I spent my childhood with him by the water. By the time I was eight, it was time for me to pitch in. In exchange for my father letting me take an occasional boat out, I began working for the business. I wanted to be out on the water as much as possible. It was the first place where I felt free, other than in the alleyway with that basketball.

To have time to hoop and surf in the summer afternoons, I took the opening shift, arriving at 7 a.m. With only the early morning company of seagulls, I would rake the beach, scrape barnacles off the sides of the boats, and refuel the boats for that day's renters. Understanding the importance of consistency and presentation in his business, my dad was perfectionistic in these tasks and expected me to uphold a standard of excellence as his employee. I grew up working with an attention to detail and feeling the pride that comes from executing tasks with diligence.

That same diligence applied to my shooting and basketball preparation, which had now become an obsession. In seventh grade, I made the junior high team, and it was the beginning of my dream's fulfillment. Although I mostly sat on the bench, I would do anything to play, and I increased my work ethic as I prepared for high school. When I arrived at Corona del Mar High School at 5 feet 3 inches and 104 pounds, I was undersized even as a guard. Fortunately, those years of perfecting my shots in the alley made me a great shooter, and that silky shot earned me a spot on the freshman roster. When I grew six inches during my sophomore year, I started to get minutes. By my senior year, I was 6 feet 2 inches and leading my team in scoring.

Yet, I was comparing myself to my best friend, Greg George, a football player, who was a highly-ranked linebacker and tight end in Southern California. Greg was raised for the game as his father Ray was a long-time coach at USC and the first player from a Catholic high school in Los Angeles to play in the NFL. As an assistant coach, Ray helped lead USC to the 1962 National Title and a Rose Bowl win with a perfect record. As the head coach of Texas A&M, he beat a Bear Bryant-led Kentucky team before returning to USC from 1972 to 1974 to help the Trojans win two more national titles.

As we grew up, it became clear that Greg would reach his dream and follow his father to a roster spot in the Trojan lineup; however, my dream to play basketball at UCLA was almost unreachable because of my physical stature. I was a good high school player, but was playing out of position. Nonetheless, I began to get attention for my shooting skills from college recruiters, including USC and Long Beach State. I was only an average student, which concerned me about college acceptance. My speed limited my ability to play the guard for a team that was winning national championships. To be honest, even my own mom said I was "too slow."

I was too small, too slow, and too whatever else they said I did not have. I knew that I would have to work and find a way or make a way to get to the collegiate level. For that reason, I began to add intensive training to my basketball workout, including a basketball weight room regimen that may have matched Greg's football workout. With squats, lunges, and power cleans, I started to get bigger and stronger and my vertical increased. While Greg's competitive drive to join the gridiron greats in the lore of USC football inspired me, I did not yet have the confidence that my efforts would lead to my dream of playing at UCLA.

During the summertime, it was common for Greg to stop by Valley Boat Rentals, either in his van or on his bike. We had designed our own longboard racks on wheels that would attach to the rear of our bicycles, and we threw our 8-foot Hobie boards in and towed them behind our bikes across the ferry, which connected the pier and the Fun Zone. When the tide came in, we would catch some waves. Surfing was another great auxiliary training workout for basketball to develop body control, balance, and spatial awareness.

At night, I would shoot another 1,000 shots in my alley, training my skill in the dark by the light of the corner streetlamp. Pushing myself to new limits was exhilarating, and week by week I broke my own personal records. Though we aspired to play for rival colleges, Greg and I certainly wanted to see each other excel in our respective sports. We were just a couple of beach rats who came off the sand, pushing each other towards playing for two of the best college teams in the country.

At night, as a break from training, it was time for the games to begin. We would head to the Fun Zone, where our competitive spirits extended past the hard wood and the gridiron. Bets would be made on who could score higher in skee ball, pinball, or "pop shot" basketball. Greg might beat me at skee ball or pinball, but I was superior in basketball. Those were the carefree days of our youth when our biggest worries were inclement beach weather and what to do when the Fun Zone closed early. The surfing and Fun Zone were always planned around my training schedule, as I was driven to improve and reach my dreams.

My first recruiting contact was from USC, and when I received the letter, I was certain it was Greg playing a prank on me. But it was truly from USC head basketball coach Bob Boyd, who gave me great advice. He told me to go at my own pace and begin my college career at the local community Orange Coast College. Although it might not have been the most glamorous place to start my collegiate playing career, it turned out to be one of the best decisions of my life. Greg went to USC on a full ride, but I tempered my dreams to play at UCLA and never lost sight of that end goal. My years at Orange Coast College were vital to my career in the most indirect of ways, through the most unlikely of avenues: a woman.

Chapter 2
MEETING THE PERFECT TEAMMATE

*"Wait for your dream, John.
Wait for UCLA."*

~ **Karen Lindroth**

CF 9363 LA

Newport Beach was Orange County's center of stunning women, who lined the white sand beaches in the summer. Karen Lindroth's beauty and presence was remarkable, well beyond my reach. She was like no one I had ever seen or met. First of all, she was captivating, with striking eyes that immediately caught my attention. On top of that magic, she combined kindness, wisdom, a perfect 4.0 GPA in contrast to my solid C+ average, and she loved the water as much as I did.

Most notably, I had no chance due to our initial introduction. During my senior year, my team played her school, Newport Harbor, in a local Christmas tournament. After a big performance, my team-mates knew that I would get the MVP award and dared me to kiss the tournament queen, who was presenting the trophy. It was a challenge, and like most challenges, I accepted. As I went up to receive the trophy, I threw my arms around the redheaded tournament queen and kissed her on the lips. Karen saw this little episode and was astonished. She thought I might be a little aggressive or perhaps a little crazy, and this high school stunt left her skeptical.

Two years later, I saw Karen's song leader team practicing on the sideline of my basketball practice at Orange Coast College. Song leaders are not cheerleaders. Their emphasis is on dance, personality, and presence. I was instantly drawn to her powerful presence and impressively high dance leaps, so I made a deliberate effort in warmups to miss a shot that might roll towards her across the court. It was a perfect miss, and by design Karen picked up the ball. To my surprise, she looked disgusted as she tossed it back to me.

At the risk of being distracted from practice preparation, I rolled it towards her a second time and was greeted with the same look. I reasoned, "We're both from OCC, so can we please be teammates out here?"

She shot back, "Don't roll that ball back here again. You're the guy with the sloppy award kiss."

It was then that I put the pieces together from that darn kiss. I figured I was done and replied, "She said it was sloppy?"

I had no idea how to recover from that until a teammate of mine, who was dating one of Karen's fellow song leaders, conspired to set us up. In view of the sloppy kiss, Karen was hesitant at first. If that wasn't enough working against me, I also had a suspect reputation of being a partier in high school and an arrogant "jock." She didn't know my character, and her tenderness was slow to recover. Thankfully, after a little convincing from her friend, she decided to give me a chance. She agreed to meet me at a friend's party, and in advance I decided to just say less.

I approached her, shook her hand, and just said, "Hi Karen, I'm John." The touch of her hand was better than the touch of the basketball, and I'm sure I held on long. Karen looked at me differently. The thought crossed my mind that she felt sorry for me, considering the pathetic kiss and that pitiful ball rolling stunt with my longing eyes. I reasoned that maybe in those eyes she could see that I was lovestruck.

I was surprised when she agreed to drive me home. I decided to ask her out the very next night. She smiled as she said, "Sure, I'll meet you at the Orange Coast Library."

I was caught off guard with excitement and responded like a guy who needed the library as I replied, "Cool! What's a library?"

Karen replied, "It's a quiet place where we can get something done."

I thought her reply was meant to be suggestive and said, "Cool, see you there after practice." I felt a renewed excitement that made my heart race and picked up my pace on the drive home.

It was all work with her, and I didn't force it. As the library lights started to dim at closing and the green banker's lamp on the study table acted as a virtual mood lamp, I stared over my book to see her glance at me. There I was again with my reckless lips taking a shot at a kiss. She shut me down cold but with a smile in her eyes.

I was a college kid, and this realization that she was earnest about a study date was disappointing at first. But that evening was an important turning point for me. I realized that part of the reason I was enamored with Karen was due to the indescribable determination that she had in every facet of her life. I knew I needed what Karen had, and I wanted it to rub off on me. With a score of 0 for 2 in our date success rate, I thought I better show some class and waited for her in the quad with flowers. I asked her one last time, "Can I meet you at the library again? I promise I'll sit at the far end of the table and not distract you." She agreed.

She encouraged me to take my academics more seriously, almost by default. We were together constantly, and she was constantly studying. This second date at the library was the beginning of Karen's powerful impact on my life.

Through these long hours at the library, I learned how she developed this incredible drive, and I became a welcomed distraction for her.

After I proved myself on our third library date, I asked her to go sailing with me. Since she was from Newport and loved the water, I figured she would be comfortable on a sailboat. I thought it would be a romantic date, and I was ready to show off my sailing skills. I knew of a spot my dad used to take me to where the water was clear and dolphins could often be seen.

She was excited at the prospect and asked, "Should I pick you up in my sailboat, or should we take your dad's?"

Little did I know that she had been sailing since she was a child. She sailed right up to our dock and was surprised to see that I had brought a picnic basket with dinner.

"You just scored points, John," she said as she kissed me on the cheek.

We sailed, and I talked endlessly about hoops as if she cared. It seemed as if she did care, for some reason. I had already been captured by her undeniable beauty, but I began to fall for her heart when I finally shut up and said, "I'm sorry, Karen. Tell me your story, starting with how you got your own sailboat."

Karen began, "Well, John, I loved your basketball stories. To answer your question, I'm the oldest of four children. Starting at ten years old, I began to babysit neighborhood kids to make some money of my own. I had to learn how to budget at a young age."

Her smile spread across her face as I said, "You impress me more every meeting."

"Each week, I divide the earnings into spending and savings. Where most kids spend their money on ice cream and movie tickets, I buy my own school clothes."

I interrupted her and said, "I thought you were a Newport kid whose parents gave her a boat."

She replied, "You saw my house. Three tiny little bedrooms where me and my siblings have bunk beds and share one bathroom."

She continued, "When I was fifteen, neighbors were paying me to babysit their kids when they would go away for the weekend. At sixteen I got my first job at a fashion retail boutique named The Wet Seal and saved up enough money to buy this used sailboat."

I said, "Wet Seal sounds like a great college job."

She looked right in my eyes and professed, "I just know that I want more than that, John." Somehow, I could already see myself giving her a good life.

There was a brief silence, and then she looked at me again and asked, "What's your dream, John Vallely?"

I certainly knew the answer, but I thought for a moment before declaring this dream that others had laughed at before. I didn't know Karen that well yet, but I felt safe declaring, "Playing for Coach Wooden at UCLA."

She looked at me with tenderness and confidently responded, "Let's get you there!"

At the end of our date, she sailed back towards my father's dock and was ready to drop me off. I asked, "Do you want help docking your boat?"

She nodded with a smile and said, "That would be lovely."

As we turned towards the Lido Bridge, I saw that the high tide had left only a small space between the water's surface and the bottom of the bridge. I said, "You're going to have to teach me how you fit this eight-foot sail through because it might help me dribble through tight defenders."

She smiled and said, "I think I can help you with your dribbling. Hop out." I jumped out of the boat, and I watched her lay down the mast, paddle under the bridge, and put the mast back up so we could continue sailing on.

She explained, "I don't have access to a dock, so after song leader practice I pull this from my house in West Newport Beach to the bay on a little hand trailer. Then I leave the boat in the water, tie it up, and run the trailer home so it won't get stolen. Then I run back and go sailing, so I hope you're ready to work today."

As we hauled her 230-pound sailing dinghy on its trailer to her house, she was beaming as I yelled, "You've got some good power, Karen."

"Song leaders are tougher than you know, Vallely," she boasted sarcastically.

I drove home after dropping her off and was thinking about her work ethic, her love of family, and the strength to pull her own boat every day. I already knew that Karen was special, but that day I realized she was extraordinary.

Karen had song leader practice the next day. Her practice ended before mine, so she sat in the bleachers with a textbook and then eventually just watched me practice. As my practice ended, she shouted out, "You're pretty good, Vallely. Let me rebound another hundred shots for you."

"I'd love that," I replied and realized that I had taken some good steps since the first library date. She stood under the basket and rebounded my free throws with no words. Just the sound of a swish and the sight of her eyes.

Karen performed at all my OCC games, where her presence captured the hearts of the fans and further reminded me to believe in myself. During my freshman year at Orange Coast, I averaged 20.4 points per game, which was an impressive enough statistic to attract attention from some major colleges. Tex Winter, whose "triangle offense" became famous while he was an assistant coach on Michael Jordan's championship winning Chicago Bulls teams, wanted me to play for him at Washington as did Coach Jerry Tarkanian, the Long Beach State coach who later went on to coach at the University of Nevada-Las Vegas. Tarkanian was the most creative coach in his recruitment tactic and offered a scholarship to Karen as well.

With the thought of Karen and me living in Vegas together, I was ready to accept until Karen said, "You need to wait for your dream, John. Wait for UCLA."

When UCLA started expressing interest in me at the start of my sophomore year, as Karen had predicted, and when a letter came from UCLA assistant Jerry Norman, I was walking on air.

Under the legendary Coach John Wooden, UCLA had already established itself as the dominant program in college basketball. The 1964 and 1967 squads had gone undefeated, and the Bruins had won four NCAA Championships and two in a row. He would go on to be named the NCAA College Basketball Coach of the Year six times. ESPN named him the "Greatest Coach of the 20th Century." The

Sporting News called him "The Greatest Coach Ever." The media named him "The Wizard of Westwood." He was currently coaching Lew Alcindor, who was known as the greatest college player ever and would later change his name to Kareem Abdul-Jabbar.

Suddenly, there was a piece of mail that came from his office. I was aware that they sent endless letters to potential recruits, but this looked like a real signature from Coach Norman, and that was enough for me.

While Coach Wooden's success on the court was unmatched, his teachings extended far beyond the realm of sports as he wanted to educate on a greater scale than the hardwood.

Although UCLA was the most successful program trying to catch my eye, I questioned how I would be able to help them. I wanted to play for a great team, but the operative word was "play." This was certainly something that I had to consider.

My coach, Bob Wetzel, said, "John, I know UCLA is recruiting you, but maybe it would be best to pick the school where you know you can play significant minutes."

I replied, "You know I can shoot, Coach, and they need a shooter to keep defenses from collapsing on Kareem."

He countered, "But because of your size, John, one of the challenges of jumping from junior college to Division One competition will be the transition from being a six-foot two-inch forward to a guard among the taller, faster, and quicker players at the top level. I'm not sure you can do that."

"Well, Coach, how will I ever find out if I'm good enough to play at the highest level at a powerhouse like UCLA if I never even attempt it?"

That was the end of the conversation. I knew UCLA would have to see me play. I was scrappy as a small kid, and the toughness I maintained to get my shot off as a freshman in high school stuck with me. Even after I grew and doubters said I couldn't achieve something, it just made me more eager to try and take risks. I knew I didn't have the most talent, but I could shoot a jump shot and make it under pressure. When the game was on the line, I was going to take that last shot.

Any lingering doubts I might have had about contributing to Coach Wooden's UCLA team were dispelled when I averaged 25.9 points per game my sophomore year at Orange Coast College. I had convinced myself that I could produce at the next level, and I was confident that I could make a valuable contribution to a team that was already at the height of its power.

With a lifelong dream to play at UCLA, you can imagine my joy when on day one of my sophomore season at Orange Coast College the schedule was passed out, and a game versus the UCLA freshman team was highlighted in red letters.

Up until 1972, the NCAA would not let freshmen compete in varsity games no matter how dominant they might be. Even majors would schedule games against anyone they could find. With Kareem on the freshman team at UCLA, they easily defeated the UCLA varsity reigning two-time champs 75-60 in an exhibition game.

Suddenly, every practice and every drill spent on the court that season was in preparation for that moment at UCLA, in hopes that I might be seen by the legendary Coach John Wooden. I added more shooting, more dribbling, additional speed and agility work in the sand, and a relentless conditioning program.

Game day came, and I walked into UCLA's Pauley Pavilion arena with wide-eyed wonder. It was everything that I imagined it to be in my dreams, except I wasn't really there yet. The championship banners in the rafters told me all I needed to know. I had to be at my best that day. The song leaders arrived early and were warming up. When Karen saw me enter, she just nodded at me with a look that said, "You got this!"

As I began to shoot around, I saw Coach Wooden enter through the tunnel with assistant coach Jerry Norman. They took a court side seat, and I was in awe. With his horned rim glasses, dark suit, and starched white shirt and tie, Coach Wooden resembled a professor that had just come from the classroom to teach life lessons on the court. Coach Norman, who played at UCLA for Coach Wooden ten years earlier, was in his team sweatsuit and appeared as if he could still suit up for the Bruins.

Coach Wooden began to watch his team warm up and watch me make fifteen shots in a row from the free throw line. It was as if I was making shots in the alleyway with this dream.

The game began. I hit my first shot from deep. I was ready. It was a back-and-forth between myself and UCLA's Curtis Rowe, and I was in the zone.

All the while, I sensed Coach Wooden's gaze was on me. Although I felt the weight of his critical glare, I relied on the technique that I had worked so tirelessly to perfect.

I was grateful to have Karen there as she understood the impact of this moment for me. Yet, in spite of the confidence she gave me, I tried not to make eye contact with her because Coach Wooden might not understand why I was shooting stares at the song leaders. I heard her voice as she shouted, "Nice shot, John! Shoot that again." I kept shooting.

It was a fast-paced game, and I found that my speed work on the beach had prepared me. It was a fierce battle that went to the final seconds. I hit a deep jump shot, and my point guard said, "Good shot, Money Man!" That's what they started to call me at Orange Coast College. We were only down by two points, with time for one more possession. I knew I could tie the game, but we fouled Curtis and sent him to the free throw line. We lost by four points. It was a tough loss, but to score thirty-five points on UCLA's highly regarded freshmen was the game I needed.

The thrill of the performance was overshadowed by the disappointment I felt, as I walked by Coach Wooden and Coach Norman, who glanced at me but said nothing. I assumed that they were unimpressed or I wasn't the player they needed. They were the top team in the country, and I should have known that they could easily recruit High School All-Americans. I looked out at Pauley Pavillion for what I thought would be the last time. I took my time to grab my warmup jacket from the bench and paused to listen to the Pep Band play "Hail To Westwood" before rejoining my teammates. With anxious thoughts flying through my head, I shook it off and approached Karen, who shrieked with excitement, "You were amazing, John. You belong on this court!"

It helped that this beauty in a song leading uniform noticed me and the work that I put in to get there, but the approval I needed was from Coach Wooden. I boarded the bus and shifted my thoughts back to playing for UNLV.

Chapter 3
PREPARATION

"I will prepare myself and then perhaps my opportunity will come."

~ Coach John Wooden

By the time a letter from UCLA arrived a week later, I had already stopped thinking about my dream. I was unaware that the NCAA prohibits coaches from speaking to recruits, which was the reason Coach Wooden and Coach Norman avoided me that day.

When Coach Wetzel called me into his office after practice and handed me an official letter of interest from UCLA signed by Coach Wooden, I was so excited that I broke into a UCLA "Eight Clap." I took the letter straight to Karen and then to show my mom who, despite her initial doubts about my potential as an athlete, was thrilled.

Karen was applying to transfer to UCLA at the time and commented, "Looks like we'll have to add some more library hours." I looked at her confused and said, "You know I love the library with you, but what does basketball have to do with the library?" She shot back, "I checked on this requirement for you so you would be ready and found out that students in the athletics division are only eligible for acceptance upon the condition that, along with the coaches' approval, they currently have and will maintain a GPA of 3.0 or higher."

I looked up at Karen nervous but determined. Even with her previous academic assistance, my 2.9 GPA wasn't up to UCLA's standard. This worried me for a moment, and Karen reassured me, "You can do this, John." I looked once again at Coach Wooden's signature, which was a handwriting that I would become very familiar with over the course of my life, and said, "Let's go!"

I removed the letter from UNLV, hung the UCLA letter in my locker and looked at it every day before practice. I knew I would do whatever it took to play for this man. Whether I chose UCLA or not, I was certain this would push me towards my personal best. When Coach Wooden and Coach Norman scheduled a recruiting visit at my home in Newport, I was waiting in that alleyway when they showed up, swishing shots with nothing but net at my garage basket just as I had dreamed. It was hard to believe that they were there. We joined my family and Karen in my living room. Coach loved and respected Karen from the start, especially after I told him she was the catalyst for my rising grade point average. Given Coach Wetzel's reservations, I knew it was important to see where I stood in their roster plans, so I brought it up with Coach Wooden. "I'm honored that you have an interest in me, but what do you think of my chances of playing at UCLA, Coach?"

He responded, "There will be no guarantees, John, just the chance to compete."

"That's all I ever wanted, Coach," I replied in earnest, and I think it was what my parents expected to hear.

My mom took it a step further as she said, "John's college coach doesn't think he's quick enough, Coach Wooden."

Coach responded, "There's always going to be someone taller, faster, and smarter. None of that matters, Mrs Vallely. What does matter for you, John, is your planning, preparation, practice, and performance, which will determine your opportunity. Your playing time will be a by-product of that effort."

Coach wanted competitors and fighters, and he also made it clear I would have to apply for admission and be accepted to UCLA on my own merit. I was grateful that Karen had prepared me. Karen said, "Coach, I will deliver this player to you with the necessary GPA and the mind of a student that is ready to learn." Coach could only smile.

Surprisingly, it was the stringent grade requirements that created an opportunity to fall in love with Karen without realizing it. After I agreed to follow her on the path towards this elite academic university, she began to coach me in my academic career. We signed up for several of the same classes the next semester, and Biology was one of them.

One day after class she handed me a yellow field trip form and said, "We're going on a field trip for biology on Saturday to Joshua Tree. It will get us extra credit."

I replied, "Extra credit? Who does extra credit?"

She said, "You do if you want to go to UCLA".

Again, "Let's go" was the only answer necessary.

The next day we went on a big school bus to Joshua Tree with the biology teacher. Instead of surfing, practicing, and partying, I spent my weekend studying trees in the desert.

In addition to the extra credit assignments, we spent countless evenings writing my application statement and studying for my tests. I started getting A's. When I opened that first report card and saw that A- in the top right corner with a 3.0 GPA, I made a copy right away and mailed it straight to UCLA admissions. It was only with Karen's help that I was able to elevate my GPA and chase my dreams. When the letter came from UCLA's admissions, I took Karen out sailing. It was another perfect evening, and I brought her favorite ice cream from Wright's Ice Cream Parlor. When she asked what the occasion was, I said, "Just for helping a jock like me." Excited, I pulled out an unopened letter from UCLA and ripped it open. "Congratulations" was all we needed to see.

Elated, she threw her arms around me and rejoiced, "You did it!"

"No," I stressed. "We did it."

Karen pulled an envelope from her purse that was already opened. I already knew she had been accepted and excitedly asked, "When do we leave?"

With the approaching transfer, I knew we needed to discuss our future. It made me nervous to consider this life at twenty years old. I shifted the conversation back to my letter from UCLA, and we just sailed and enjoyed the beauty of that Balboa Island purple sunset.

I knew that Karen wanted to graduate from UCLA and ultimately get married and raise a family in Newport Beach. My dreams had been defined by the basketball goals that we had pursued together, but she made it clear to me that her dream of building a family was her first consideration. She wanted to attend UCLA in the fall with me but did not have the money for tuition. I tried to convince her to reapply with financial aid, but by this time she had risen very fast at The Wet Seal, where she continued to be promoted to becoming the youngest manager at the company. She decided to stay in Newport Beach, where she excelled and moved up. Although she hoped for a future with me, she was not ready to follow me to UCLA. We were only dating at the time, and with strong wisdom, she had valid questions about my intentions. We were both glad that I would only be an hour away and could still visit one another on weekends.

I wasn't certain about my future with Karen yet, but I was certain that she had changed mine. I packed for UCLA and looked out at this beautiful Balboa bay that molded my life, and I reflected on its "man made" creation, which I had learned about in Geology class that spring. I knew it was the perfect place to mold a dreamer, a stargazer, and a rainbow chaser like me. Starting out as a mudflat surrounded by a swamp, this bay required dredging millions of tons of silt on the way to this picturesque destination island with canals, a ferry, and a bridge. Sometimes life is a swampland that needs a visionary and a bulldozer. Karen had seen through my unactualized life and saw beauty which could be developed into its potential.

I knew I would miss her and this Bay Front view, but it was time to leave for Los Angeles and the magical campus of UCLA that was tucked away in the college town of Westwood.

Chapter 4
THE
FOUNDATION

"Success is a peace of mind which is a direct result of self-satisfaction in knowing you did your best to become the best that you were capable of becoming."

~ Coach John Wooden

I couldn't wait to get on the road and be a part of UCLA basketball. The energy hit me as I exited the 405 while blasting Marvin Gaye on the radio and drove into Santa Monica. I breezed down Pacific

Coast Highway, passing the world famous Santa Monica Pier. I then passed a strand of roller skaters, surfers, and beach volleyball legends along this 22.3 mile bicycle path that bordered California's "second best beaches" only to Newport Beach, of course. Turning onto Sunset Boulevard, I continued through the winding canyon of the Pacific Palisades and its Santa Monica Mountains, with vast, sweeping coastline views of the ocean below and lined with palm trees and wildflowers all around me. I was enchanted by these 13 miles of magic, which continued inland through Brentwood, one of the most luxurious and polished neighborhoods in the world to live. I passed the quaint Bel-Air Sands Inn, a sanctuary where our team would stay the night before home games so as not to be distracted. From there, it was a short trip down the hill and into Bel Air, where Rolls Royce and Porsche convertibles sped past me on their way to the West Gate of Bel-Air at Bellagio and gated multi-million dollar mansions sat directly across the street from UCLA.

I marveled at the thought of movie stars living on one side of Sunset and sports stars on the other as I turned off Sunset into the campus, with dreams of stardom. I took a right turn on Westwood Plaza and another right on Charles Young Drive and continued down Westwood Boulevard and onto Weyburn Street at Broxton. This is where fans lined the streets at the legendary Fox Theater hoping for a chance to see the walk-by of Jack Nicholsen and Dennis Hopper at the premiere of Easy Rider. I took another right turn onto Gayley, passed the UCLA Medical Center, and arrived at the center of this majestic red-brick campus. This was the legendary arena that would stand in the center of my life and define my future: Pauley Pavilion.

I was no stranger to the Southern California lifestyle, but I was just a blue-collar surf kid who cleaned movie stars' boats. Suddenly, here I was on the verge of stardom myself. I traded my surf shorts for the team-issued UCLA basketball gear and showed up on day one at the Mecca of college basketball, where I was face-to-face with the biggest basketball stars in the city. Coach John Wooden and Kareem

Abdul-Jabbar, an unstoppable pair at UCLA, were coming off back-to-back National Championships and its best season ever.

I was stepping into an unstoppable success that the world of basketball had never seen. Before we even got to know one another, I knew all about Coach's success on the court, which had to be attributed to more than just his understanding of the game. He was instilling values into his players that made them mentally and physically strong, which extended well beyond the court. I was ready for some unique wisdom but nothing like what I would experience on this first day.

I was greeted by Kareem, who was every bit of 7 foot 2 inches tall, lean and muscular, well-spoken, and bright. He had a slight tilt in his shoulders, either out of habit to get through doors or to appear shorter and less awkward. Kareem extended his hand and said, "Heard great things about you, John. I'm Kareem."

He approached the other players and said, "This is John Vallely, a great shooter who broke eighteen scoring records and will open up our offense this year."

A couple players introduced themselves. Their names were Ken Heitz and Sidney Wicks. Kenny Heitz was 6 foot 5 inches, cocky, and appeared nerdy and academic with his thick "coke bottle" glasses despite his strong frame. Sidney Wicks was 6 foot 9 inches with a tight Afro and a too-tight T-shirt that showed his strong frame. He would become my year one roommate and a great friend.

I shook hands with them and extended my hand to Curtis Rowe, who had a look that matched his personality: abrasive. At 6 foot 7 inches and 225 pounds, he was a force for opposing defenders to guard and had a great presence on the boards. I had battled Curtis in the Orange Coast vs. UCLA game and had played well enough against him to be noticed by Coach Wooden, so I knew he was well aware of me. "I'm John Vallely."

Curtis responded, "Like JV? That's where you'll be, man, on the JV squad."

Players howled at the statement, and I was surprised but knew it was a competitive group. I shot back, "I believe I dropped thirty-five on you right here at Pauley, didn't I, Curtis?"

Unimpressed by my rookie confidence, the veteran players snickered and Curtis continued.

"That's right, Rookie, or should I call you Money Man? But we got the 'W,' and I got forty-two!"

Luckily, Lynn Shackelford, a typical tall, lanky, suburban white guy from Burbank with a sharp shooting lefty gun, sensed the tension and stepped up.

"I'm Shack, and this is Steve Patterson, Bill Sweek, George Farmer, Terry Schofield, John Ecker, and Sidney Wicks, another JC transfer."

I was glad the team tension was broken up as we heard the voice of Coach coming down the hall. Players suddenly started betting.

Shackelford said, "Five bucks that Coach uses a Whitman quote."

"Ten bucks it's Shakespeare. Definitely Shakespeare!" Kenny responded.

Kareem said, "No man, it's George Moriarty for sure."

Coach entered with his signature blue and gold warm up jacket and tightly laced Converse Chuck Taylor high tops. He sat down, made eye contact with every player in the room, and he quoted George Moriarty that day.

> "Who can ask more of a man than giving all within his span.
>
> Giving it all it seems to me, is not so far from victory." [1]

Kareem, who knew Coach as well as anyone, just smiled. Suddenly, Coach began to remove his shoes and socks. I was puzzled but transfixed. His high tops would be the beginning of my classroom. After his feet were bare, he looked up at us and said, "First things first. Please take off your shoes and socks."

I immediately began to untie my laces as Kareem muttered, "Not the shoes and socks again, Coach."

Coach dismissed the statement from this great veteran, and once we were all barefoot he continued, "Men, the most important part of your equipment is your shoes and socks."

With the precision of a surgeon, he demonstrated exactly how we were to apply the socks.

"Hold up the sock and work it around the little toe area and heel area. Pull it up over your toes and pull it up tightly to eliminate any wrinkles."

Some veterans were rolling their eyes and others were snickering. I was hanging onto every word as he continued, "I want absolutely no folds, wrinkles, or creases of any kind. Now open your shoes so that they slide on and do not undo the work we just put in to keep our socks wrinkle-free. Pull the laces tight. Pull them again. tighter. Tighten it up snugly by each eyelet. Then you tie it, then double tie it."

After he finished tying his shoes, he stood up and said, "The game begins from the ground up. You see, if there are wrinkles in your socks or your shoes aren't tied properly, you will develop blisters. With blisters, you'll miss practice. If you miss practice, you don't play. If you don't play, we cannot win." I had never seen anything like this before. It sounded eccentric, but I wanted to soak up everything I could from this legend.

Coach continued, "You will find that success and attention to details—the smallest details—usually go hand in hand. I want to win championships, as I'm sure you all are interested in; however, if you want to win championships, you must take care of the smallest of details."

Next, the winningest coach in college basketball announced, "Now having said that, I will never use the word 'winning' again."

If that wasn't wacky enough, he then handed us what looked to be a page from my geometry class with a giant triangle on it. The same image was also drawn on the chalkboard behind him. I looked down at mine and immediately saw at the top in large writing, "The Pyramid of Success." In the middle of the page was a large pyramid composed of fifteen "component blocks" that, before I had the time to read each box, Coach began to explain. It was as if he was another professor on campus as he pointed at each box and explained their definitions.

"Look at those blocks. There's fifteen of them that, when working in cohesion, add up to success. The bottom row is the foundation of the whole pyramid. The foundation begins with Industriousness, which is hard work. There is no substitute for work. Worthwhile results come from hard work and careful planning. Then comes Friendship, Loyalty, Cooperation, and Enthusiasm. Friendship is a powerful force that comes from esteem, respect, and devotion. Work at it. Don't take it for granted. Be more concerned with loving than being loved, giving than receiving, and being a friend rather than having a friend. At the center of the foundation, Loyalty is positioned between Friendship and Cooperation. Loyalty is the glue that holds them together and the force that forges individuals into a team."

I was hopeful that maybe I would become a part of this glue. He went on, "Cooperation is finding the best way rather than having your way. Finally, Enthusiasm is the igniter that turns hard work into Industriousness."

He then pointed at the next level up on the pyramid and said, "Work your way up here to Self-Control, which is practicing self-discipline and keeping emotions under control. Alertness is being aware of your surroundings and eager and willing to learn from them at all times. Initiative is the ability to make decisions and think alone, preparing thoroughly in all ways. Intentness is concentrating on achievement with determination and persistence, resisting all temptations which will affect your preparation. After that comes Condition. You know we will be a well-conditioned team on the court, but I believe it is impossible to attain physical conditioning without first achieving mental and moral conditioning."

I felt the stare of Curtis Rowe, who was staring at me and snickering. I was relieved when he finally spoke about a term I knew was related to basketball. Coach said, "At the very center of the Pyramid is Skill, which is the ability to perform quickly and properly, executing the fundamentals with detail. Team Spirit is an eagerness to sacrifice personal interests of glory for the welfare of all."

When he said "Team Spirit," I was immediately thrown back to Newport Beach and the life teammate I had just left behind. A little homesick, I allowed my mind to stray, but I couldn't day dream for long as Coach kept going.

"If you do these things, you rise up to these two blocks of Confidence and Poise. I don't believe you can have Poise and Confidence unless the other blocks are in place. They happen naturally from proper preparation. Ultimately, all fifteen blocks in the pyramid are necessary for finding our personal best in Competitive Greatness, which is having a love for a hard battle and knowing it offers the opportunity to be at your best when your best is required."

Coach had me now. I knew I would have to battle every day to get in this lineup. My game with Curtis already gave me confidence that I could battle here.

The lesson continued with a teaching about joy as he claimed, "There is a joy that comes from being involved in a pursuit that challenges your mind, body, and spirit."

You can't argue with Coach, but the joy of winning and playing on National TV and getting to the NBA had to be pretty cool. I was hoping there wouldn't be a quiz as the definitions continued with the mortar, the blocks that hold everything together. These were Ambition, Sincerity, Honesty, Adaptability, Resourcefulness, Reliability and Integrity.

When Coach Wooden got to the top with Fight, Integrity, Patience, and Faith, I was drawn in but confused.

He went on, "Excellence requires patience. Success requires patience. And yes, I believe we must have faith that things will work out as they should when we do what we should."

Then Coach spoke of prayer, which really made this meeting mystical.

He continued, "There are many things that are essential to arriving at true peace of mind, and one of the most important is Faith. This is belief without evidence, which cannot be acquired without prayer."

I couldn't be the only one that day wondering what prayer had to do with excelling in college basketball? After all, I had gotten this far with a very concrete work ethic which included years of training, skill work, and studying in the library. We were college guys thinking about the game and this championship.

Then as Coach was done talking about faith, he said, "There is no guarantee that living out all of the ideals will bring about the desired results."

He called the highest point of the pyramid "The Apex." There, in Coach's own handwriting, was written the definition of "Success," which he recited. "Success is a peace of mind which is a direct result of self-satisfaction in knowing you did your best to become the best that you are capable of becoming."

He looked in my direction, where I probably appeared bewildered and overwhelmed with information, and continued by saying, "Success is giving one hundred percent of your mind, body, and soul to the battle. The only one who will ever know if you've achieved your personal best is you."

He looked around the room and made eye contact with every player as he would often do. I looked down quickly so he couldn't pierce me with his thoughts again. When I looked up he stated, "When you get to that level where you're at peace about your effort, you have found success."

It was perplexing, but what if there was an element to my game that I had been missing? What else could I learn from this legend? As I looked around the room, half the players looked skeptical like me. Back-to-back championships had been won, but peace of mind was the goal? I could only hope this peace of mind would help me when I missed fifty percent of my shots and twenty percent of my free throws, which were the average numbers for a great shooter. I thought the only thing that could have made this meeting more atypical would have been to talk about love.

The meeting ended, and as I walked out towards the court, a paper airplane whizzed by my head. I picked it up, and it was The Pyramid of Success hand-out. I turned and saw veteran players were molding them into paper planes and tossing them at the rookies. I stepped over them and onto the court. With my perfectly tied shoes, I was ready to battle!

From that day forward, I was ready to relearn everything I thought I knew about the game of basketball and life. Coach had mentored the best teams and the best players ever, and they trusted him. Even on that first day, the Wizard of Westwood didn't need the whistle hung around his neck in order to command his team.

Everyone on the team had been a star player in high school. To be honest, I found the competition in the practices to be better than many of the games we played in my previous season. That's not to say the competition from other schools wasn't worthy, but I was in awe to be practicing with and against Kareem, one of the greatest players in basketball history and the most dominant player in the country at the time. With amazing physical strength, great passing, a soft touch jump shot, defensive blocking skills, and his famous skyhook, he was unstoppable. He accepted me and took me in as a teammate. Improbable as it was, the kid whose own mom thought he couldn't make it at this level was now playing alongside the greatest college player in the country.

Before the organized practice began, we would warm up by shooting free throws and working on individual weaknesses. The free throws were to my advantage, and my teammates saw my shooting skills right away. Next was footwork that included stutter steps, jump stops, pivoting, and defense.

Coach Wooden walked through both groups, and he was on me right away about my off ball cutting. He said, "You don't need to be fast to play fast," but I knew that he needed me to play fast. I tried to make up for my lack of speed by maneuvering and cutting, and he was quick to call me out. He said, "Be clever, John, not fancy. Clever gets you open, but fancy brings ridicule." He was right, and the other players were now laughing at my goofy footwork.

Then it was the stop-and-turn crossover drill. Coach walked through the lines as we would dribble, jump, stop and pivot. "You have to be a good dribbler here," he said. "The stop jump is made with the feet wider than the shoulders, knees bent, hips low, and the head up. The turn is on the inside foot, with the outside leg swinging back, and good balance maintained."

I was up next, and I turned wrong.

"Inside foot, John," said Coach.

This was so mechanical for a freewheeling beach shooter. I was never taught the importance of fundamentals this way. I did it my own way more than once and got frustrated. I could tell Coach was about to come at me with more mantras.

"Do things the way you have been told so you won't have to be told every day. Correct habits are only formed through continued repetition of the perfect model," he said.

Then Coach broke us into two groups.

At one basket, the guards worked with assistant Denny Crum, who would go on to his own legendary head coaching career at Louisville. We worked on the pass from guard-to-guard-to-forward and the UCLA cut. At another basket, assistant Gary Cunningham worked with the centers and the forwards on delivering the pass into the key.

I was having a tough start, and I was disappointed that Coach Jerry Norman, who believed in me, had left UCLA. He was the lead recruiter and the architect of UCLA's swarming press defense of many great teams and would move on to a successful career in the investment business. It was Coach Norman who created this opportunity when he found me and convinced Coach Wooden to recruit me, and I would always be thankful.

After the drill work, Coach would bring all the players back to one basket and work on the play first, without defense. Then the defense was added, and he would correct all of the fundamental errors. The offense was complex and different from Orange Coast College, where I would come down the floor and shoot. At UCLA, the plays would involve a chain of cuts, screens, passes, catches, stops, and pivots, all intended to free a particular player for a high percentage shot. Coach stressed the synergy of the team with quick passes and immediate attacks to get open shots as the defense shifted to look inside first and then to the perimeter.

Coach demanded execution through learning, drilling, and practice of fundamentals, for it was true that the chain was only as strong as its weakest link. A lapse in any fundamentals along the way would likely render the play ineffective. I realized that I needed to learn his system, or I would be the weakness. For a moment, I realized that Coach was right. I was certainly slower and less athletic, with less vertical power than these players I was practicing with that day.

Coach was up and down the court that day with his mantras, and they were always timely. Coach believed in an up-tempo style and liked to extend the offense against pressure defense in a fast break, emphasizing passing before dribbling and getting the ball to the sideline cutters in a 3 on 2.

We ended with a 3 on 2 and then a 2 on 1 drill. It was my turn, and I knew this was my chance to show my shot against pressure. I dribbled the ball down the court. I accelerated past Shackelford, and I knew that I belonged there. Kareem closed out, then I jump stopped and felt that ball come perfectly off my hand as I put up a shot that I had made thousands of times. Kareem swatted my shot deep into the bleachers, and suddenly I realized there was much more for me to learn, especially about the value of the team.

As Coach came storming down from the top of Pauley, where he was known to watch practice, he admonished me by saying, "If you cannot obtain a good shot, pass back and set up. You can't just heave up any shot, John."

Curtis Rowe was back in my face again and said, "I see you, JV squad!"

With that taunting, I knew I needed to make that shot. The next time down the floor, I decided to defy Coach Wooden and shoot the same shot even though Sidney was open on a cut. This one was nothing but net. Nonetheless, Coach was back down the bleachers again and exclaimed, "Goodness gracious sakes alive, John!" This was as bad as it could get with him. "Keep your eyes up and look for the sideline cutters."

Coach called us up, and I was waiting for him to admonish me for shooting instead of passing or relay some other basketball related wisdom. Before I knew it, he was reciting a poem by heart called "How to be a Champion" by Grantland Rice.

> "You wonder how they do it,
> You look to see the knack.
> You watch the foot in action,
> Or the shoulder of the back.

But when you spot the answer,
Where the higher glamours lurk,
You'll find in moving higher,
Up the laurel-covered spire,
That most of it is practice,
And the rest of it is work."

With Coach, I was always surprised. He might teach basketball technique or give us motivation. He might rebuke us or give the gift of wisdom that we would take for a lifetime. His hard correction was never lost on me, and the poem that day was a welcome sound and reminder to keep working.

Kareem pulled me aside on the way to the locker room and consoled me by saying, "John, don't sweat this, and don't worry about Curtis. He knows you can shoot."

Then Curtis interrupted us briefly to say, "That was a pretty nice make, Money Man."

Kareem carried on, "He sees your talent. Don't sweat Coach Wooden's 'goodness gracious' either. He knows you can play. But just so you know, when four players touch the ball and the fifth hits a layup, you will see him smile."

I kept my eyes up and started to distribute the ball. It was good to see Coach Wooden smile.

After my first few weeks of staring at nothing but textbooks and my teammates' faces, Karen's surprise visit was a welcome sight. We jumped in her VW convertible and drove down San Vicente to Santa Monica.

It was a warm late afternoon in November. Karen turned on the radio. Marvin Gaye's "Ain't No Mountain High Enough"[2] came on, and she started belting out the lyrics. She glanced over at me while she was driving as she sang, "'Cause, Baby, there ain't no mountain high enough, ain't no valley low enough, ain't no river wide enough to keep from getting to you, Babe."

I took over with my air microphone and sang, "My love is alive, way down in my heart. Although we are miles apart, if you ever need a helping hand, I'll be there on the double just as fast as I can." It felt great to have this love that was always there for me.

We drove by the beach and marveled at the hustle and bustle of the beachside city of Santa Monica. It wasn't quite as peaceful as Balboa Island, but we took on the energy of the west side. We pulled up and parked at the Santa Monica pier. It wasn't the Fun Zone, but I was glad to jump on a ferris wheel with her once again.

As we rose above the park at the top of the ferris wheel, I saw the magnitude of creation differently. The ocean, the mountains, and maybe Coach Wooden's faith had started to enter my thought process.

We moved towards the sand, and as I laid out the blanket, I had one thought on my mind: feeling her arms around me again. As she leaned her head against my shoulder, I said, "Could there be a more perfect place in the world?"

Karen replied, "You make it perfect."

I saw Karen differently than I had ever seen her. At nineteen years old, I saw her as a beautiful song leader. At twenty, I saw her as a team-mate who could help me on my path to UCLA. Now, I saw her as a partner who could change my life.

In her typically thoughtful way, Karen had a picnic basket and said, "I brought your favorites from home: a turkey sandwich from Wilmas, fresh fruit from Dad's Deli, and a Balboa Island classic – a frozen chocolate banana."

The peaceful sound of the waves calmly crashing made me slow down from the frenetic pace of my new life and routine. It was a full two hours before she asked me, "How are your test scores, John?"

I said, "Basketball practices are hard, Karen, and taking up my time to study. But I'm getting A's and B's."

Excited, she shouted, "Really?"

I replied, "Believe it or not, with help from the school's tutors for my more challenging classes, but I miss our teamwork and am homesick for the sight of those soft library eyes."

Karen said, "I miss your eyes too."

With Karen, I could sit for hours in the OCC library, which explained the meteoric rise of my GPA. Without her, I was staring out the window of the UCLA Powell Library. The view of the quad's activity was enough to hold my attention, but I knew I needed Karen. I needed her motivation in the books and on the court. I missed my sideline song leader, but I was grateful to have her close enough to come and cheer me on from the UCLA stands.

It doesn't take much to get motivated when you're surrounded by championship banners and All-Americans, but there was nothing like her influence on my gameday spirit.

On the last day of her visit, Karen pleaded with me, "Take me to Powell Library 'cause I can't believe you are going to a library on your own."

Karen had brought her book backpack with her that weekend. Sure enough, we found our way to a table in the stacks, and she was surprised when another student greeted me by name. There was no romance needed there that day. I was all about that GPA now as much as she was and brought my GPA up to 3.2 that year. I briefly glanced over my textbook and she smiled but said, "Keep reading." It was her library sessions that had filled me with hope and a dream that was coming true.

When it was time for practice, she walked me back to Pauley Pavillion, where we walked by all the past championship trophies, photos, and the jerseys of the former UCLA greats including Walt Hazzard, Gail Goodrich, Lucius Allen, and Keith Erickson.

Karen paused for a moment and stared in silence at the photos of these NBA players and pointed at a blank space. "I can see your picture hanging right here, John." I was grateful for her confidence, but I knew this journey would have to begin with some playing time.

We walked past Coach Wooden's office and stopped to say hello. Coach was glad to see Karen again and said, "Come sit in on practice today, Karen."

As we warmed up that day, he spoke to Karen. I was grateful for those moments she and Coach spoke. He would become a part of Karen's life as he did for many player's girlfriends, wives, and families. Just the sight of Karen's beautiful face smiling from the bleachers at practice that day inspired a greater performance from me. I had begun to combine the mindset, discipline, and conditioning to play at the pace that Coach expected from his guards. Make no mistake about it. We ran hard, and we ran fast.

In addition to all of his foundational teachings, I was learning the complex UCLA offense, which wasn't easy for a guy who came down the floor and fired up shots in junior college. I began to comprehend its pacing, timing, strongside-weakside balance, passing, screening, and cutting. I was gaining precision, flawless execution, and a faster pace, along with the structure to get open and make open shots.

As Coach pointed out earlier, I couldn't just heave shots up. What made Coach's offense brilliant was that it forced us to think and execute precision in scenarios that were determined in a moment by the defense's reaction. He taught us to follow our instincts and to respond to challenges in real time as we must do in real life. The individual decision-making made it hard to defend. I had to learn how to pass and create passing angles instead of dribbling. I also had to discern when to take risks and shoot the open shot.

It was a process of learning complex UCLA cuts and ball reversals and executing side post game and ball reversals, the flex post offense, and the side post offense.

While pacing up and down the court with energy, Coach would serve up another one of his favorite maxims, "The man who is afraid to risk failure seldom has to face success."

Sometimes I had to come off Kareem's pick and shoot, and sometimes I had to give up shots in order to get higher percentage shots. I had to learn when to take risks.

The practice ended that day, and I approached Karen within an earshot of Coach. "What did you think?" I asked.

It didn't take Karen long to respond by saying, "I think when you execute the UCLA cut towards the basket, via Kareem's back screen, if you don't get the pass, you have to continue harder to the corner."

Coach knew she was valuable and pointed at her as if she gave an assist. Then he approached her to say goodbye and said, "Karen, sit in on practice anytime and keep reminding John to 'Move, move, move'!"

That night, she was drilling me on the Pyramid hand-out and she was quizzing me on the blocks. I asked her, "Do you think faith makes sense in this Pyramid?"

She looked at it for a moment and replied, "John, it seems to me that faith is the glue of what your team is doing. It is believing that the cutter will be open, the screener will give you an open shot, and faith will help you knock down that twenty-two foot jumper." She was clearly brighter than me.

The next day, it was more instruction for my raw skills that needed refining. We started with a series of shooting drills without a ball.

I tried to cover my laughter as Coach instructed us to warm up with a series of shooting drills without a ball, and Sidney said, "Talk about faith."

Drills included change of pace, direction drills, and in-place jumping drills with no ball. We also did imaginary tipping drills to quicken and increase our spring.

Coach explained, "John, it's not how high you jump, but when you jump and the position of your jump that will make you competitive at this level."

When we split up for one of Coach Wooden's competitive shooting drills, no one was laughing as I was on fire. We divided into competitive groups of five to shoot mid-range and set shots or jump shots. The first group with fifty makes would win, and the losers would run dribbling a ball. That alleyway was short in the middle, and I was forced to shoot ten to fifteen footers. Guys were competing to get me on their team after that day.

Coach also taught me about adjustments that day. Within the high post or low post offense, there are plenty of options available to create a variety of shots. Options include down screens, guard reverses, double screens, crossing with the other guard, or faking the cross and flaring to the same side. I was ready.

The one that made Coach notice me involved passing to the center, which is a good idea when you have Kareem, who liked to give back to me when I had a hot hand on the perimeter. The precision of our offense was vital within the proper boundaries of individual play.

At the end of practice, Coach brought us up and pulled out a card from his wallet. With a quick shift from the game, he was talking about heaven and prayer again. His game-time mindset was focused on perfectionism towards the game, but he loved teaching life lessons.

He explained, "My father Joshua Wooden taught me to read every day in my youth, and he taught me to read the Bible. He gave me this card at my graduation. On one side is a verse by Henry Van Dyke." Coach recited it by heart.

"Four things a man must learn to do
If he would make his life more true.

To think without confusion clearly,
To love his fellow man sincerely,
To act from honest motives purely,
To trust in God and Heaven securely."

On the other side of the card was what he called his "7 Point Creed." He continued by memory, making eye contact with every player including me. The first three points of the creed were:

1. Be true to yourself.

2. Help others.

3. Make each day your masterpiece.

Number three made sense from a perfectionist who demanded mastery from his players. Then the balance of his teaching shifted again to thoughts of the Bible and prayer. The next points of the creed were:

4. Drink deeply from good books, especially the Bible.

5. Make friendship a fine art.

6. Build a shelter against a rainy day.

7. Pray for guidance, and count and give thanks for your blessings everyday.

Coach added, "But realize that material blessings and the accolades you will receive from this game will not be the source of your peace. I'm not a theologian and respect everyone's views here, but I hope that you will read the Bible and pray as my dad encouraged me."

I was counting my blessings for the chance to be at UCLA but, like the Pyramid of Success, prayer had escaped me. Prayer was what we did at the free throw line or on test day. I wanted to believe in God, but I had not sought Him sincerely. The Bible was another book on the "to do" list. We all wanted a masterful performance, and I was determined to master basketball.

That mastery under the coaching of John Wooden would elevate my game quickly, but I was surprised when Coach took me aside four days before the first game of the season and said, "John, you have prepared yourself well for this season, and you have grown in skill, team spirit, and confidence. What do you think about starting against Purdue in the opener?"

My heart was racing. "Coach, isn't that what it's all about?" I instinctively blurted this out while realizing that this was a short-sighted response to Coach's ears. Yet, I was pumped and had advanced from the last of the possible starting guards to the coveted starting rotation.

From that day on, Coach's team room and court teachings would begin to take a hold of my life. I was living that dream that Karen told me to wait for. When I called to tell her that I was starting, she exploded with excitement and jumped into the 405 traffic for the first game, which was a true sign of her commitment.

After playing in the Houston Astrodome in front of a crowd of 50,000 the year before, UCLA was at the epicenter of the college basketball universe. Needless to say, this first home game at Pauley Pavilion and all the other games afterward would be sold out. This added to the rush of playing at home.

As we took the floor and the sea of blue and gold stood up and cheered, it was thunderous. I thought of my path here from the Orange Coast College game on this court just a year earlier and considered there might have been some type of guidance as the 7th point on Coach Wooden's Creed suggested.

From the opening tip-off of that game, I saw my opportunity to show that I could contribute at this elite level. Purdue was preoccupied with stopping the seemingly unstoppable Kareem. To achieve this, the Boilermakers played a zone defense to keep their defenders close to the basket. The collapsing defense opened up the perimeter for me and, just like that offense we worked on, Kareem kicked that ball out to me–the "too slow shooter"—and I scored nineteen points. I was elated to show Coach (and my teammates) that his faith in me was warranted.

The L.A. Times had a nice write up about me, and my confidence surged. The media caught onto my nickname, "Money Man," which made me happy.

The campus of UCLA and Westwood Village was an electric place to live my first year, with a pedestrian energy that could only be matched by New York City. Streets were blocked off on weekend nights. The team liked to hang out in The Village where the scene was iconic and home of Stan's Donuts, Tower Records, Westworld Arcade, and Dillon's Nightclub. I walked down Weyburn Avenue past the Holmby Clock Tower, the official indicator to let you know if you were under the curfew.

The end of the block was the heart of the action where the Fox Village Theatre anchored the corner of excitement. Movie viewer lines stretched around the block, and a bar called Nite School provided a trusted alibi. We could always say, "Yep, we're at Nite School again."

Our team's success was drawing media awareness around the players, and it was fun for me to be recognized by the student body and fans as I walked through campus, and airports.

Despite our success, I found that it wasn't always glamorous behind the scenes. My arrival on campus coincided with the turbulent times of the late 1960s. Martin Luther King had been assassinated, giving way to the release of pent-up rage and riots that broke out across the country. I relied on the game for social guidance as it provided both an escape from the turmoil and insight into the reasons behind our country's racial conflict. Pauley Pavilion, the site of our practices and games, was my sanctuary. The locker rooms, buses, and hotel rooms served as my extended classroom. While Coach Wooden taught me about life, my teammates taught me about our society.

After the games, the team would go back to the Bel Air Sands Hotel and watch replays of the game on television at 11 p.m. One night, during a casual recap session, Kareem and I wound up having a particularly deep conversation about basketball and life. I asked him, "What is it like to have so much pressure on you, Kareem?"

He scoffed and said, "Watch on the road and in the airport terminals. You'll see, John, as bystanders react and gawk and ask me foolish and awkward questions because of my height. Off the basketball court, I have daily reminders that as a seven-foot, two-inch black man, I am displaced. I don't fit in."

It broke my heart that Kareem, who had been kind to me as an outsider rookie, felt displaced. It was impossible for me to comprehend, so I tried to bring some positivity. I said, "But UCLA loves you, Kareem."

"Not off the court," he countered. "In Westwood Village, many ignore me."

"What about students?" I asked.

"Believe it or not, John," he said, "some move away from us when we sit down in the cafeteria. Even people I thought were my friends have rejected me. There was a time in eighth grade when I was walking down the street in New York, and I saw one of my best friends, a white kid, on the other side of the street. I called out to say 'hi,' and this supposed buddy, with some provocation from the other white kids, turned on me completely ignored me."

I didn't know how to respond except to say, "I'm so sorry, Kareem."

Kareem continued, "If that wasn't bad enough, another time my high school coach tried to motivate me in a game with the same language. Can you imagine a coach berating you and calling you names to try to make you work hard? It hurts, John."

I could only shake my head at the foolishness of this intolerance and bigotry. He looked at me with disappointment in his eyes as he responded, "I'm not treated like a star, John. When we play at some schools on the road it's really bad. At Cal Berkeley they shout things like, 'Hey spearchucker, where's your spear?'"

When Kareem said that it filled my heart with terror and anger and helped me understand his anger.

I responded, "I'm just a white kid from Newport Beach, and I've never experienced anything like this. I don't care if you are black, green, or yellow, and I don't care that you are seven feet tall. We are brothers, Kareem."

It sounded like a line from a film on race relations, but I made it known that I valued him for his character and dignity and appreciated his sensitivity, which went much deeper than the public could ever see.

We embraced this personal and special interaction that night and we agreed on our collective purpose as I heralded, "I feel like we are both here for something bigger than UCLA, something bigger than basketball, and something bigger than either of us Kareem."

Kareem nodded and said, "Let's fight for something greater than trophies, John." I know now that we were right.

I was truly moved by his willingness to share his experience, and I will never forget those moments of trust and understanding. Those moments helped me to grow and better appreciate Kareem as well as my other teammates. I suspect that the candor and honesty was unique for the time.

The conversations I had with teammates were a special part of my UCLA education and became lessons that I wouldn't trade for anything. Additionally, I learned about empathy and respect through the sport. Although I couldn't always feel the pain of their struggle, I could at least share their ideals and share their dreams in the words spoken by Dr. King in his speech.[3]

> "I have a dream that my four children will one day live in a nation, where they will not be judged by the color of their skin, but by the content of their character. I have a dream that every valley shall be exalted, every hill and mountain shall be made low. The rough places will be made plain and the crooked places will be made straight. And the glory of the Lord shall be revealed and all flesh shall see it together."

I'm certain that mutual understanding and acknowledging differences, which was part of Coach Wooden's belief in team spirit, held his teams together at a time when other school basketball programs might have experienced a divisive spirit. On the court, the playing field was equal because we were judged by our performance. I loved giving that ball to Kareem in the low post, where he could score at will, and he often gave it back to me.

Kareem was dominating. He scored twenty-four points per contest, followed by Curtis Rowe at 12.9 points. I was third on the team in scoring, averaging eleven points per game, which was more than I could have expected when I was shooting shots in that Balboa Island alley and hoping only for a chance to wear the UCLA jersey one day. All the wins were thrilling, and beating teams on the road was action packed. The win at Cal on March 1 with the final score of 84 to 77 felt like a special victory against the racism that shouted at Kareem. On that night, The "valley was exalted and the mountain made low."

As we entered the NCAA tournament, it was thrilling for an athlete that came from a junior college arena. At those NCAA games, the crowd experience was a massive step up from high school sports and

The Pyramid Principle

junior college, where there's no pageantry of a marching band, a pep rally, or the adulation of fans. The motivation I felt on those earlier courts was found within myself and not from the crowd. In the Spring of 1969, the chance to play on a national stage and on national TV was another wish fulfilled. In that first regional game, we ran through the field and beat New Mexico State with a score of 53-38. I had ten points and five rebounds. In the game against Santa Clara, with the final score of 90-52, I went five for five from the field.

We were on to the national semifinal game. As usual, we would dress forty minutes prior to the game and Coach would tell us to sit quietly, get off our feet, and act business-like and serious. When Coach brought us up, there wasn't much pre-game rhetoric or pep talks. This game was no different, and he went over the game plan. Then he gave us a simple lesson that I could never realize was going to last my lifetime. He said, "All I expect from you is to be able to answer to yourself when the game is over."

The opportunity that I had prepared for, not just during the season but for my entire life, finally presented itself in March Madness on March 20, 1969 in Louisville, Kentucky. Drake was a high scoring team and had won ten games in a row to get to that game. They were focusing all of their attention on stopping Kareem by double and triple-teaming him. Instead of running the offense through Kareem, as we normally did, Coach Wooden cleared the left side of the court for me and let me go at my defender. Kareem was kicking out passes to me, and I was on fire. I already had twenty-seven points when they fouled me and sent me to the line with ten seconds left, and we were only up by one point with the score sitting at 83-82.

I stood at the free throw line, and it was as if all the blocks of the Pyramid began to make sense as I moved towards competitive greatness. I could feel the culmination of the industriousness involved in training, the basketball skill work and execution, the thousands of shots in a Balboa Island alley, and the work ethic I learned from Coach and my father. I also felt the full impact of Karen's friendship and support while teaching me the academic intensity needed to get me into UCLA.

I hit those two free throws with confidence to seal the win in an 85-82 victory.

I finished nine for eleven from the field, eleven free throws, and a team high of 29 points, even outscoring Kareem.

Athletes never plan for extraordinary things to happen, but the great ones simply prepare the best they can by practicing the fundamentals like doing their homework then hoping for the best when it comes time to apply the skills acquired in practice. I realized success that day because I performed my best when my team needed it most and rose to the occasion when Kareem had three defenders on him. Coach Wooden taught me to step up to be my best, which was about to be required on bigger stages for higher stakes. The teamwork I brought to a UCLA win was more significant than statistical accomplishments, but the media launched me to stardom that day.

After the game, when we were getting on the bus, Kareem turned to me and joked, "John, you're making it hard for me to win the 'Most Outstanding Player' award of the tournament. Kareem was a great teammate, but he knew who he was and so did everyone else.

I said, "Just giving my best, Kareem. Thanks for the assists."

We entered the Championship game against Purdue, and we easily defeated them at 92-72. I chipped in fifteen points towards our win, and Coach Wooden's thoughts on work were realized. He had said, "There is no substitute for work. Worthwhile results come from hard work and careful planning." While this was UCLA and Coach Wooden's third consecutive National Championship, it was a first for me, and I felt even taller after I climbed down from the net cutting.

Kareem grabbed that MVP award with 37 points and 20 rebounds. I was selected to the Final Four "All-Tournament Team," which made me an Orange County hero.

Karen was at the Championship game, and after we won, I searched the crowd to find her. I knew that I could not have accomplished any of this without her. Karen taught me to learn, grow, and push myself to make my goals a reality. We sat there separated by cheering teammates and fans, but all we could see was one another with appreciation and pride. Though this was a moment of celebration, it wasn't time to rest just yet.

I threw my arms around her as the crowd cheered and the band played, and I shouted, "Thanks for believing in me!"

Karen preferred to place her face right next to mine and whispered, "You're easy to believe in, John. One championship down, one more to go."

She was right. I still had one more year to go, but I knew I hadn't arrived yet. Maybe it would take another championship win or making it to the elusive NBA. I was about to find out why Coach would never define success as winning or accomplishments.

Chapter 5
OFF-SEASON

*"It's what you learn after you know it
all that counts."*

~ *Coach John Wooden*

I decided to switch up my intense basketball training. After all, one of the blocks of The Pyramid was Initiative. I thought it would be good to add volleyball back into my training during the summer, which I loved anyway. I soon found myself playing in a highly competitive beach volleyball arena. Most importantly, basketball and volleyball have a shared history. Many athletes made great strides in both sports, including UCLA's Greg Lee and Keith Erickson. I decided to throw my hat in the ring among these elite players. Basketball helped me develop many of the skills I would need, so it made sense. I wanted to be on the beach as much as I possibly could that summer. It's a quick drive back down Sunset Boulevard to the Santa Monica Pier, where the competition was elite as was the vibe. The sun and surf brought the beach bodies and parties out in full force during the summer. After the last match was played, the bonfires on the beach began. It was a carefree life without the rigors of the academic load, but the habits I learned during that summer volleyball season kept me disciplined in my off-season.

I first started playing volleyball in highschool. After re-entering the game as a college junior, I picked up right where I left off. My basketball skills transferred to volleyball quite well. I had great hops and had impeccable ball control that helped with passing and setting.

My friend Greg came to visit me around this time at UCLA. I recognized the familiar honk of that van. I jumped in for that beautiful drive down Sunset Boulevard to Santa Monica Pier, where I was looking for a relaxing day of surfing and a beach bonfire party. We didn't say much, with the exception of fighting over the radio songs. He wanted "Get Back" by the Beatles, and I kept changing it to "What's Going On" by Marvin Gaye. We finally agreed on "Hot Fun in the Summertime." We belted out the lyrics, "End of the spring, and here she comes back. Hi, hi, hi there. Them summer days, those summer days, hot fun in the summertime, hot fun in the summertime, hot fun in the summertime, hot fun in the summertime. We were happy."[4]

We arrived at the beach and pulled up to the sand. I jumped out and grabbed my board from the back of his van as he shouted, "Surf's up, John!"

This beach was beautiful with palm trees swaying, soft sand beneath my feet, and the sound of the waves lapping up on the shore. As we walked towards the shore, I looked back at Greg and saw that he was wearing his brand new USC football jersey.

I said, "You want to be seen in that jersey in West L.A.?"

He replied, "Yeah, I'm proud of this. Why?"

I said, "They call USC a 'private school' because no one wants them to know they go there."

He laughed and said, "No matter what you think of the Trojans, let's see who catches more waves."

We paddled out, and we fought for the first wave. I was up first. We surfed for a few hours. I felt a good burn in my legs and in my lungs. I was grateful that we got to come out onto the waves together as surfing connected me to the balance Coach spoke of, and Greg knew it helped his football training as well.

Greg got up and beat me to a wave. On this wave that he would normally master, he got wiped out off the board. My glee at beating him was instantly replaced with confusion and concern as he paddled to the shore. "You alright, man?" I asked.

"Just been having some tightness with my knee, John," he answered. "But I'll push through."

"You owned me in that first set, Greg."

"I know! It felt good, but it can lock up on me anytime."

"Man, Greg, don't leave me to surf by myself for the rest of the summer."

"No, John, I'll surf with you in a knee brace."

"Good, Greg. I need you to get to the next level."

"I needed you today, John!"

"Always here for you, Greg."

Greg sat down for a minute to let his knee recover, and I jumped into a volleyball game with a couple of buddies from UCLA. Ron Von Hagen was on the other side of the net and saw my skill that day. He asked me to team up with him, which was an honor as Ron was the "Babe Ruth of Beach Volleyball" and on his way to the volleyball Hall of Fame. Ron also attended UCLA, where he initially played three sports including freshman basketball. Following his father, who was a basketball All-American at UCLA, Ron became a student of the

Pyramid of Success and took Coach Wooden's principles to the sand. Ron won his first Open at Laguna Beach in 1964. From 1964 to 1978, he played in 120 tournaments accumulating 62 wins, 33 second place finishes, 7 third place finishes, and set 33 records. No other modern male beach athlete has come close to that winning percentage.

Known as "Von Muscle" for his physique, he was a fierce competitor with perfect technique. I had to learn some things from this master like I had from Coach Wooden. Ron was insightful to understand that two-man volleyball technique had some passing magic just as Coach Wooden's offense involved technical passing.

He instructed me, "Just like you got used to passing to the sideline cutter on the fast break, you'll get used to passing to me."

"How did you know Coach got on me for that?" I demanded.

He said, "Had to do my homework on you, John. I watched all your game films too. Which reminds me, you have to work on your speed before next season."

"Yeah," I responded. "But did you see my hops this season?"

"Yeah, you have the ability to get that shot over an outstretched defender. Can you use those same hops to get up and block a six-foot-six-inch volleyball player?"

After a long day of practice, Ron took out a container of what looked like a chocolate shake. It turned out to be raw liver. I said, "You're different, Von Hagen" and pulled out a peanut butter and jelly sandwich on white bread and a vanilla shake. I knew that the vanilla ice cream from Wright's Ice Cream Parlor could do more for me than anything Von Hagen could be drinking.

Blessed with a genius IQ and an exact memory for statistics, Ron also taught me about the mental side of beach volleyball game. He had every opposing player's stats stored in his head. He knew the players' game by game weaknesses, such as who to hit to and when. He also knew my weaknesses, and I spent that summer working to eliminate them.

Ron was a very special part of our summers. We were on top of the beach world. Ron was a testament to the power of condition, skill, and intentness. He was competing with players who were better at each of the skills individually and better hitters or defenders technically, but no one could hold a candle to Ron's relentless drive to win. We played in the days of "side-out" scoring when you could only score while serving, which created endless matches that would go into the dark and take every ounce of energy. In a sport that's known for its beauty at the beach, it was also grueling in the heat of the sand and the sun. I would add all these lessons to the character building, and I'm certain that Von Hagen made me tougher physically and mentally.

Ron's gifted memory would also bring his timely recall of his own learned Coach Wooden rhetoric. He was quick to say, "Hasn't Coach Wooden's mantra on work ethic hit you yet, John?"

"No," I responded. "I've been trying to get his poetry lessons right."

"I know he gave you this one after the Henry Van Dyke poem. 'Goals achieved with little effort, are seldom worthwhile or lasting.'" He was right, and my effort increased.

Ron and I had an equal dedication to competitive greatness. We had a perfect season winning the four open tournaments we entered on the way to the Manhattan Beach Open, which was the Wimbledon of Beach Volleyball. We ran through the field and then faced future Hall of Famers like Henry Bergman and Larry Rundle in the finals. It was a back and forth to a tie match in Game 5.

We huddled for a moment. He looked at me with his steely-eyed game time glance and said, "Be ready, John. This game point is yours."

Ron gave me a perfect set, and I rose up high above the net and placed that kill right down the line, beyond Bergman's reach for the win. I looked right next to where Karen was sitting and cheering, where I was often glad just to look over and stare at her beautiful face.

To this day, our plaque stands at the Manhattan Beach Pier for the 1969 Manhattan Beach Open Champions. It's not the same stage as winning NCAA Basketball Championships, but I'm proud of it. It was one more event that forced me to train and play beyond my limits.

As remarkable as that summer was, when the fall came around I knew it was time to get back to basketball full time. The summer was a fun time, and my time playing beach volleyball with Ron was invaluable. He is another one of the teachers in my life who modeled true competitive greatness, and he empowered me to take on this next season with a quicker step and another two inches on my vertical leap.

I spent one weekend back at home, and Greg and I had to get one more shot at skee-ball in the Fun Zone before we graduated the next spring and adulthood set in.

The score was tied. Greg rolled a 50 and shouted, "Hope you're feeling lucky!"

I lined up my shot and set my stance as I instructed, "Never get too high, never get too low."

Greg laughed at me as he taunted, "This isn't the free throw line versus Drake, John."

I rolled a 100 for the victory and mocked him with his USC "V" sign as I said, "Next year when you visit, I'll give you some Coach Wooden Pyramid mindset work."

He laughed as he asked, "I don't have to learn poetry, do I?"

Chapter 6
"THE TEAM WITHOUT"

"Winning takes talent, to repeat takes character."

~ *Coach John Wooden*

Coach would often say, "Winning takes talent, to repeat takes character." The focus is not on the result but getting there from the inside out. I knew that this upcoming season would require me to play an even more important role in both. I came to UCLA to be a part of a special Bruin team at a unique time. I was able to experience greatness firsthand by playing with the great Kareem Abdul-Jabbar. I was also able to participate on a team that would have to rebuild its very foundations against all odds.

Kareem was now on the Milwaukee Bucks and was the NBA's number one overall draft pick. He was averaging 28.8 points and 14.5 rebounds per game for a team that would win the NBA championship in his second year.

Lynn Shackelford was drafted by the Houston Rockets and had moved on to the NBA as well. As a result of our key losses, Coach Wooden sometimes referred to our distilled group as "The Team Without." All the pre-season prognosticators could talk about was the players that we were missing.

By all media estimations prior to my senior year, this new team would mark the end of the UCLA reign atop college basketball. Coach would name me captain of this team, and it would be a chance for me to prove that I could lead a group of underachievers to greatness.

In year two, I moved off campus and lived in Westwood on Pico Boulevard above a Chinese restaurant, where Karen and I had many date night dinners. It was a time to slow down, reconnect, and simply talk face to face, which we didn't get to do often with 58 miles between us. I decided that I would announce the news that Coach had named me as captain with a fortune cookie.

After the waiter brought the check along with a tray of fortune cookies, I opened mine with a playful jest first and read it aloud, "The object of your desire comes closer."

Karen placed her head on my shoulder and said, "Can I keep this?"

I laughed and gave her the real message which actually read, 'Enjoy the meal; buy one to go.'

She played along as she opened hers, read it, paused for a moment, and looked me in the eyes and said, "Look how far you've come."

I quickly responded, "Really? That's amazing because Coach just named me his team captain."

I pulled out a carefully folded headline from "The Daily Bruin," which I had cut into the size of a fortune. She unfolded my headline and read the words out loud.

"Senior John Vallely Named Captain of 'The Team Without.'"

She turned to face me and grasped my hand tight. Far from the days when she looked at me with suspicion at the library, I could see pride in her eyes. "I really am so proud of how far you have come," she gushed.

Then I grabbed the real fortune off the table, and we both laughed as I read the real message which said, "I cannot help you for I am just a cookie."

The times like this with Karen took my mind off the pressure. Though the team was anxious amidst negative projections, Coach Wooden was unphased on media day as he said, with microphones in his face, "We will put a competitive team on the floor as we always do."

It was great to see Sidney again after the summer. He had grown his hair out with long sideburns and a mustache. Fully aware that this look would not fit well with Coach Wooden's clean-cut standards, I said, "Coach isn't gonna' like that."

Sidney broke out in his perfect Coach Wooden imitation, which he was known to do for humor in team gatherings, and said, "Sidney, you know my rules about long hair and facial hair. It interferes with your vision and gets in the way of your ball handling."

I laughed and enjoyed the comic relief as we both entered the team room and I greeted my teammates. There were returning veterans Curtis Rowe, Steve Patterson, Terry Schofield, and John Ecker to name a few. The key players were new to me, and I introduced myself to six foot four inch Kenny Booker from Long Beach Poly and Long Beach City College. I then introduced myself to six foot one inch guard Andy Hill from Westwood and an average of 27 points per game at University High. Next I greeted six foot one inch guard Henry Bibby from North Carolina. As Kareem had done for me, I said, "Great to see you again, Henry."

As we heard the familiar sound of Coach in the hallway, I knew big trouble was on the way. I inched towards him in anticipation of what was about to happen. We sat down, and everyone sat up tall. I knew Coach was going to come in teaching life lessons, but this started differently than I anticipated.

It took one look from Coach to size up Sidney's new look and say, "Sidney, you know the rules about facial hair."

"I do know the rules about facial hair, Coach, but you don't have 'the big guy' this year and you're going to need me."

Coach said, "Sidney, we can use you this year. What team will you be playing for?"

Players covered their snickering, and Sidney resisted for a moment with a statement of his rights.

Then Coach said, "Sidney, you are absolutely right. You do have the right to wear your hair any way that you want, and we will miss you!" He then got serious and said, "You have 15 minutes till practice starts. You need to get into Ducky's office, cut your hair, and get back in time for practice or you will not be playing for UCLA this year."

Sidney responded, "You don't like me, Coach" and moved quickly out the door and ran upstairs to our trainer's office to use his clippers.

We held our laughter and knew Coach would be irritated if we didn't gather our composure for his shoe tying demonstration. For a moment, I got caught up in the entertainment of watching the reactions of the rookie players as Coach removed his shoes and socks in front of the team. I was right on track with him this year as I started to understand the player that I would be from giving attention to details would be the player I was on the basketball court.

I was more attentive this year to his instruction as it related to the socks at the little toe and the heels, knowing that it really did affect the fast paced running and cutting. As we pulled the lace through the last eyelet, we were ready to get on the court, and the veteran players began to rise until Coach held up his hand. We sat back down.

We knew what was coming next as "The Pyramid of Success" hand-out was being passed around. Coach approached the black board. I didn't want to look up from the page this year because I was certain that someone would be poking fun at the talk to come.

Coach spoke in detail about all those elements again, but for some reason I heard Coach talk about the mortar called "fight" differently than the year before. Maybe I recognized this team without Kareem would need to fight, scrap, and battle harder.

His explanation fueled me for a breakout season.

"Fight is a determined effort to do the very best we can do. On the basketball court, fight is measured by hustle, diving on the floor for a loose ball, sprinting to fill a lane on a fast break, taking a charge, picking up a missed defensive assignment, or stealing the ball from an opposing player. When we have fight, we are ready to respond by standing our ground. We are quick, but we don't hurry. We make fewer mistakes because we have the level of intensity under control. A player with fight has a contained and focused passion. I often hear others talk about getting up for a big game, but no game should be bigger than any other. Players with fight can't get up any higher for an important game because they get up high for every game. When you step onto the floor this year, give everything you have to give, whether it's for practice, a scrimmage, or the championship game. There's no such thing as losing when we've made the best effort to do the best we can do. If we use our fight and determination to do our best, success will take care of itself."

That was his introduction to the apex and the definition of success. This year it included a poem.

By this time, I knew that Coach loved a poem as much as he loved to talk about offense or defense, but he explained that this simple verse, along with his father's advice, is what grew into his own definition of success. He recited:

"At God's footstool to confess,

A poor soul knelt and bowed his head. I failed, he cried, the Master said, Thou didst thy best, that is success."

It became a lifelong guide for Coach, and the people who were fortunate enough to become his students would learn this definition by heart, including me.

And as he read the definition, I was reciting it in my head along with him.

"Success is a peace of mind, which is a direct result of the self-satisfaction in knowing that you did your best to become the best you were capable of becoming."

I was hoping that this peace would provide relief from the pressure put on us by the media. It was a sense of peace I once thought you could find through winning, but this year I understood that hard work would be needed for self-satisfaction and rewarded with a peace of mind.

Some did an eye roll at the Pyramid of Success hand-out, but I had begun to understand that this set of fifteen "blocks" working in cohesion led us to Coach's desired outcome.

Yet, "faith through prayer" still seemed misplaced to me. I could comprehend that faith in this setting might be faith in your teammates, faith in your process, or faith in your performance when the game is on the line. However, I had yet to grasp Coach Wooden's faith through prayer.

I would come to understand that I was gifted by God's hand, and everything I would do one day would be to His glory. At the time, however, this seemed just as folksy as some of the players felt about the shoes and socks tutorial. The blocks that forced me to work, commit, and strive for greatness were an extension of my upbringing in the game.

At the same time, faith on this practical level led me to dismiss the doubters who said we could not repeat without Kareem. Faith also brought Sidney to trust his coach, and he returned under thirty minutes all cleaned up and shaven. He was welcomed back on the court with our team intact.

Evidently, the journalists who predicted a UCLA decline didn't account for UCLA's perennial success in attracting new talent. Without question, it would be difficult to replace Kareem, but we added some key talent starting with Kenny Booker, a confident player who was among the leading scorers on his high school and junior college teams. Kenny sat out his initial season at UCLA from '68 to '69, red-shirting to preserve his remaining two years of eligibility. Now he was finally ready to play.

And on the first day of practice, he walked up to me and said,

"John, I'm gonna take your starting spot."

I looked at him and said, "Good luck, Kenny. Dream on." Players who came in and looked at my skinny frame and athleticism were gunning for my spot.

I knew that Kenny was going to be an important teammate. His playful but competitive attitude would help me play the very best I could that season. As far as him taking my job that year, he didn't stand a chance. Even so, Kenny was a defensive specialist on our team. As we took the court to work on our defense, Coach taught me and Kenny pushed me to develop more offensive weapons.

Many freshmen that came to UCLA didn't understand Coach Wooden's meticulous attention to detail on defensive stance and balance. Not only was Coach talking about balance on the court, but he emphasized that the fundamentals of defense would apply for the rest of our lives.

As his lessons continued that day in a series of defensive drills, he was walking through the line drills as he recited one of his fabled sayings.

"One of the most overlooked and underestimated things in the world is balance," he said. "Basketball is a game of balance: emotional, mental, and physical. To execute the fundamentals involves, first and foremost, that you can successfully stand on your own two feet. The basic stance requires that your knees are bent, your torso is up, your shoulders are level, and the head is directly above the midpoint between your two feet, wider than the shoulders. Once you've accomplished this position, you can harness quickness. Without quickness, you have activity without achievement like kids running around a playground with a ball. You should never mistake activity for achievement."

While we held a defensive stance, Coach walked between the lines, pushing some players and bumping others in an attempt to get them off balance. "There's nothing more important than balance. Never get too high and never get too low, John," he said as he pushed me.

I regained my balance. Maybe I still didn't know everything about the game. He pushed Kenny, who held his stance still, looked at me, and announced with a sarcastic tone, "See what I mean, John? That's a starter's stance."

When Coach wasn't looking, the playful banter continued.

I looked at Kenny, gave him an imaginary shooting form, flicked my wrist, and held my form until Coach turned back to our line and gave me that glance.

Coach went on, "All of life is peaks and valleys. Never let the peaks get too high, and don't let the valleys get too low." Even though Coach was weaving through the whole team and pushing each player, I felt as though he was speaking directly to me as he recited the statement that I would carry with me for the rest of my life.

Coach continued, "Someday you are all going to face a great challenge. Are you ready to regain your balance in the face of any obstacle?"

I was a college kid at the prime of life, and I filed this particular life statement with attention to detail. One day I would need this very statement more than I could ever realize at this moment.

What I didn't understand then was that Coach was molding me for a life that would have balance and power on the court, a life that would have crumbled without this foundation, and a life that could stand at the peak with humility. As Coach would recite, "Talent is God-given, so be humble. Fame is man-given, so be grateful. Conceit is self-given, so be careful."

More than the need for humility, Coach would give me the power to climb out of deep valleys.

There was more as Coach continued, "I want to help you learn to work hard in three areas of life. Certainly, I want you to get the most out of yourselves physically, but I also want you to learn to work hard mentally and emotionally. This requires you to have discipline. In order to harness your physical ability, you must be emotionally and mentally balanced. Physical conditioning, of course, is needed to play this game but also to gain control in other areas. Adversity is your asset. You cannot control your circumstances, but you can control how you react to them."

Then it was a flurry of drills with and without the ball including defensive slides, jump stops, and dribble stops. I brought that fight and stance to practice that day and took charges, dove for loose balls, and filled lanes.

We broke down for a session of shooting. Sidney broke into his best Coach Wooden imitation at this point. "John," he said, "One day you will need this stance."

He intentionally stood like a cartoon character with an exaggerated stance, and I made a shot right over his head. "You're too low," I said in jest.

Coach caught the end of the banter and shot a look at me. He brought us back to work hard on his UCLA offense, with a technical masterpiece of wing cuts, back cuts, down screens, low post and high post passing, and triangles. These techniques would become even more important without Kareem.

This was my senior year, the culmination of my amateur playing days, and my chance to truly capitalize on all the work I had put in and validate all of the trust and faith put into me by Coach Wooden and my team. I knew that I needed all of it—the conditioning, the correction, the considerable time Coach spent teaching me how to move like an elite guard, and infusing life lessons into practice.

At the end of practice that day, he brought us together and addressed us. It sounded like a reference to Sidney and the haircut, but Coach had a way to penetrate the right player at the right time with the right lessons.

"I don't like you all the same. You won't like me all the same. You won't like each other all the same. The good Lord, in His infinite wisdom, made us all different. But, I do love you all the same."

The lessons got better every day.

On the way to the locker room, Sidney said to Kenny with sarcasm in his voice, "There's no way that Coach loves you the same, Kenny."

Kenny shot back, "Yeah, but he loves me better than John."

I could only respond, "That's probably true."

It was true until we started the season undefeated. I was averaging nineteen points per game and leading the team in scoring, but I was taking a fair amount of shots to get those points, which Coach continued to remind me throughout the years. Even so, Coach used to give me the simple directive, "Shoot the ball when you are open."

I had one of the most accurate shots on the team, but there was a growing consensus among my teammates that I was not only shooting but scoring too much. A teammate came to me and told me the guys were concerned. He said, "It just wouldn't look right, man, if a team with so many talented brothers had a white player leading them all in scoring."

As the team captain, I knew that I needed to respond with patience, so I humbly replied, "Let me give that some thought."

I stayed up all night thinking about what I should do. I decided not to discuss it with Coach Wooden. Although he had taken principled stands against racial inequity and boycotted tournaments early in his career that excluded players by race, Coach was not aware of some of the racial issues on his own team. He always welcomed players to exercise their constitutional rights to free speech, but Coach also believed that nothing should overshadow the team's goals.

As I had learned from Kareem, I wanted to consider the racial climate my black teammates were facing at the time. I went to Powell Library and read through some newspaper and magazine articles that might give me wisdom.

It was staggering to think that it took two decades after UCLA alumni Jackie Robinson broke baseball's color line for integration to change the face of college basketball.

At the start of the 1960s, it was still common for teams in major conferences to have only one or two black players on their teams until a major milestone occurred in 1966. Texas Western, now University of Texas-El Paso, started five black players and beat Kentucky's all-white team in the National Championship game.

By the 1970s, the majority of players on many teams were black. Not every moment can be as dramatic as the Texas Western-Kentucky game, but the movement had found its way to me.

At Orange Coast College, my team had only one black player named Clarence Oliver from Laguna Beach. It was the first time I had played with a black teammate. By my senior year at UCLA, I was in the starting lineup with three African-Americans, and a fourth black teammate came off the bench.

From the beginning of our time at UCLA, Coach Wooden emphasized that our team would be a collaborative effort. Sometimes we would do something to help a teammate. Sometimes a teammate helped us. Function took precedence over feelings, and cooperation required a willingness to adapt in order to improve the spirit of the team. Coach told us he hoped the players would develop friendships along the way, but he recognized that we were all high-spirited athletes and that friendship might not always be possible among such a collection of proud and accomplished competitors.

Maybe I didn't quite comprehend how the leading scorer's race would make a difference. The more I listened and observed, the more I realized the importance of being sensitive to issues of racial discrimination, its struggles, and how my teammates were perceived in society. My world opened up at UCLA.

Because of my ability to shoot a basketball, I found myself in an environment where I continued to grow emotionally and intellectually while being exposed to many different viewpoints.

I was concerned that if I told Coach about this scoring situation, he would come down harshly on the team for disrupting the harmony, which would only increase the division. I also could have simply gone on playing the way I always had. I was troubled by the notion that my scoring would be an impediment to the team, and I cared that it bothered the others.

I looked at the Pyramid of Success hand-out hanging in my locker, and the cooperation block meant that I would reign in a few of my shots without anyone knowing what was happening. I could come off of a screen and pass up a shot I would have made. I could give the ball to a cutting Sidney Wicks, Curtis Rowe, or Henry Bibby instead of hitting that corner baseline jumper.

Thankfully, I had Kareem as the best example of a collaborative effort. The greatest player in college history, he could have scored forty points a game but gave up his personal glory for the glory of the team while our offense ran through him and around him. Due to his selfless play, the opponent had to guard five players.

Then I thought of Coach saying that he "loved us all the same," and I made the decision to give out some "love."

I passed the ball like "love" depended on it, and Sidney wound up leading the team with eighteen points per game. I still scored sixteen points per game, Henry averaged 15.6, Curtis 15.3, and no one ever discussed it again. Besides, the balanced scoring probably made us harder to defend. Maybe implementing teamwork was another step of "faith" for me.

I knew there was going to be more to learn, but this year's "Team Without" was winning game after game. As we moved our winning streak to fifteen straight on Jan 30, I scored twenty-five points in the second half as we upended Cal at a final score of 87-72. Similar to my development at Orange Coast, I was becoming a second-half player at UCLA and would need that 3rd and 4th quarter mentality in the next arena of my life.

The streak went to twenty-one in a row until we played Oregon and were surprised to be taken down by a score of 78-65 from a team we had beaten handily earlier at 75-58.

Coach wanted his players to be confident. We never expected to lose a game, but our rare losses gave us a chance to be honest with our weaknesses. Coach always had great wisdom in a loss. He said,

"In a season, you can get away with defeating marginal talent. In life, you can sometimes cruise through years without having to dig deep in your preparation. But eventually, something comes along that pushes you towards your fullest potential, and how you respond to each goes a long way in defining your character." He would never be more right with me, and it was a good wake-up call.

Karen was at practice the next day. By this point she was having conversations with Coach Wooden in the stands while we warmed up. When Karen was there, I practiced harder.

We had fallen short, and the excuses were beginning at practice. Players blamed each other, and some blamed themselves.

It was time for a life lesson, and Coach loved this lesson as it reminded him of his upbringing by his father and his days as a player in the game in the state of Indiana for Purdue University.

"Some of you have heard my 'Two Sets of Three' that I learned from my father. He said, 'Johnny, remember these rules your whole life.' The first set of three is about honesty: Never lie, never cheat, never steal. The second set of three is about dealing with adversity: Don't whine, don't complain, and don't make excuses."

Everyone else thought they were corny, but I wanted the moral compass of this six-time National Champion Coach. The second set of three was easier for most to understand. Its theme was to shut up, play hard, and play your best. That first set of three was lost on most guys. "Never cheat" certainly refers to integrity and doing the right thing towards others. My mindset was, "Don't cheat on the university that is paying for my education. Don't cheat on the girlfriend who gave me inspiration."

What hit me that day was this thought: "Never cheat on yourself!" It goes back to giving my best. I could look in the mirror at the end of a day and know that I didn't lie to Coach or the fans who came for an experience or to myself about my effort. I gave it my all.

The next night, we beat Stanford by thirty points with a final score of 120-84. Sidney got his press that week, tallying twenty-seven points in only thirty-five minutes. Henry Bibby added twenty-three points, and Curtis scored twenty-one points. I was genuinely happy to see those guys score and succeed, and none of us were complaining about shots.

It was time for a back-to-back match against our crosstown rivals at USC.

For only the second time that season, we lost with a score of 87- 86 at Pauley, and the team was crushed to lose this one that felt so important, especially in front of our home fans. Coach reminded us, "Study, learn from it, try not to lose the same way, and have the self control to forget about it."

When we took the court at USC the next night for the shoot around, I was glad to see my friend Greg in the stands early, despite the fact that he was wearing that awful cardinal and gold colored jersey. I was concerned to see him in a knee brace from his persisting knee problems. I went over, shook his hand, and said, "Get well soon, Greg. I don't want to beat you in skee ball 'cause you can't play in a good stance."

"I'll beat you on one leg," Greg shot back.

The rivalry between UCLA and USC is always intense, and their home crowd was ready. The banter got ugly as UCLA fans shouted, "University of Second Choice!" or "University of Spoiled Children!" USC fans chanted back, "Don't Bruin your life!"

You learn to tune it out at all the opposing arenas, and the only voice I heard was my friend Greg's loud voice cheering when I hit a jump shot. I was grateful for his teamwork that ran side-by-side with me and conditioned me to beat his Trojans with a final score of 91-78. This team that I captained had won the conference title and was the top seed for the tournament.

The media barrage began, and I enjoyed most of it.

A reporter asked me how it felt to be competing for a title without Kareem. I answered with as much humility as I could and said, "It's funny people still ask us about the challenge of playing without Kareem and about the pressure of winning. I've never really thought of it in terms of pressure. Not winning has just never occurred to me. We've always been winners and fighters here, all of us from high school to today. Winning is the only thing we know. There are no other options. Besides, we're scoring more and having fun."

I showed up to practice the next day, and Sidney had a copy of "The Sporting News" from March 7 with me on the cover. He had taped it over his face with eye holes while he imitated me shooting and quoting a previous article. "I'm the blond beach boy who steadies the UCLA back court," he said. He was a great prankster and kept the team loosened up. He finally came back to earth and said, "I'm proud of you, John."

"Proud of you too, Sidney," I replied. "But Coach said to have character and not be a character."

He laughed and shouted, "I get those confused."

We cruised through the first rounds of the NCAA tournament, beating Long Beach State at 88-65, Utah State at 101-79, and New Mexico State at 93-77. On March 16, I appeared on the cover of Sports Illustrated with Bob Lanier from St. Bonaventure, Dan Issel from Kentucky, and Jimmy Collins from New Mexico State. Sports Illustrated was the top sports magazine at a time when the sports media wasn't flooded with content, and this was beyond my imagination.

The National Championship would be at Cole Field House in College Park, Maryland against Jacksonville and the seven foot two inch All-American named Artis Gilmore, who had just defeated the number one team of Kentucky and legendary coach Adolf Rupp.

The media's pressure and expectations were high, but we focused on being our best as we did all year.

A day before the big game, we came into the gym where Gilmore and his Jacksonville teammates were going through a practice session while blasting music from a big boom box and goofing around. We took the floor and, in contrast to their practice, went through a half hour of a perfectly precise practice.

The footwork was perfect, our passing was perfect, and the fast breaks were precise. Overmatched physically, we knew we would need precision to beat them. As we stared at the imposing size of Gilmore, Coach said, "It's not the size and strength of a player; it's how he uses his size and strength."

In the first half, Steve Patterson was having a difficult time controlling Gilmore. Coach Wooden called a timeout. Sidney said, "Coach, let me guard Gilmore."

As always, Coach wanted him to play at Gilmore's side, and Gilmore was destroying six-foot-eight-inch Sidney. Then Sidney moved behind him. Coach had to trust Sidney now, as Sidney trusted Coach on the first day of practice. Sidney used all of his strength and power as he began out-jumping Artis and blocked five shots on his way to the MVP award.

It was a long way from that first day as Sidney and Coach learned how to trust each other, and I learned to trust my teammates.

Sidney had seventeen points and eighteen rebounds, Steve Patterson had seventeen points and eleven rebounds, Curtis had nineteen points and eight rebounds, Henry Bibby added eight points, and I had fifteen points. You couldn't have written a better script for team spirit.

It was the sixth of UCLA's record seven Championships in a row. Again, I was selected to the All-Tournament Team. What was most gratifying was how we defied everyone's expectations as a team. It would have shocked the sports world had we not won the championship in the 1968-69 season; but in the 1969-70 season, we played in the skeptical shadow of the sports media machine. It didn't matter that the odds were against us as we met the challenge head-on.

Coach Wooden's advice to "respect all opponents, but fear none" proved to be true in 1970 and in my approaching life battles.

As the captain, I cut the last piece of the net. I hung it around my neck, and someone snapped a photo with Coach and me. The championship trophy still reminds me that "a player who makes a team great is more valuable than a great player. Losing yourself in the group for the good of the group–that's teamwork."

As I left the court that day, I listened to the UCLA band play the Alma Mater "Hail to the Hills of Westwood"[5] one more time. I thought of my Orange Coast versus UCLA freshman game, where I was certain it would be the last time I heard it. That song would continue to have a sacred meaning to me as a player and as an alumnus. I sang a few words:

> "Hail to the Hills of Westwood To the mighty sea below; Hail to our Alma Mater
>
> She will conquer every foe.
>
> For we're loyal to the Southland Her honor we'll uphold.
>
> We'll gladly give our hearts to thee, To the Blue and to the Gold."

While I didn't fully realize the value of the education I received from UCLA and Coach Wooden at the time, I more than appreciated it the deeper I got into "the real world." His principles prepared me to conquer every foe, but first I had some major life decisions to make.

Chapter 7
"YOU MARRY THAT GIRL"

"I wish I would have put love at the top of this Pyramid."

*~ **Coach John Wooden***

After winning my second championship under Coach's brilliant leadership, it was time to think towards the future. Fortunately, the NCAA Tournament propelled me into the ranks of the top guards in the country, and my draft stock was rising. I was selected by the Atlanta Hawks in the first round of the 1970 NBA draft as the 14th pick. My family, teammates, and Coach were all extremely proud.

The path that I had taken to get there gave me peace of mind. I knew that I had done my absolute best, and it started to connect with this principle of faith I had been wrestling with.

CHAPTER 7

I had learned to jump over the high hurdles in sports and knew the hurdles of life would continue. I was aware that I played the same position as Atlanta's leading scorer, "Pistol" Pete Maravich, but after I signed my contract to play in the NBA, I was in high spirits. My dreams of playing professionally and bringing the lessons that Coach had instilled into the real world were about to be tested.

After the excitement of my future career settled, I felt my enthusiasm fade when I actually visualized the reality of moving away from California. I realized that I had a decision to make: Where does this amazing partner of mine fit into the picture?

My NBA bound teammates and I were imagining a life in the game and a life beyond it, and we were excited about the prospect of a glitzy life with glamorous women. I briefly joined in on the conversations about groupies and fan attention, but I was aware of the temptations ahead and really wanted Karen by my side for the next chapter of life.

The following weeks were filled with meetings, signings, and parties. All of these were a distraction from this big decision, but it managed to find its way back to the forefront of my mind. Though this was a time to celebrate, it was also the start of a big transition, and I wanted to give myself the proper space to reflect on the past and plan for the future. I thought through my life, career, and financial future and found no resolution. When I realized I needed help thinking this through, I only wanted one person to help me. I knew that Karen should come on this journey with me.

The next day, I asked her to go sailing with me. It was a perfect night. The sun was about to set, and I had brought a bottle of wine and my radio. We sat side by side, surrounded by the sights of the bay as we listened to the sound of waves gently crashing against the boat and the familiar music of Marvin Gaye. It was in that moment as we floated on the easy waves that I knew I could not imagine my life without her. All I could think of was this perfect life we would both have together, until I asked the imperfect question.

Flooded with emotion, I decided to ask Karen, "Will you come to Atlanta to live with me?"

I was so carried away in the moment that it almost didn't register when she replied, "Is that your best offer?" My collegiate immaturity at this time clouded my understanding of her response, and I didn't know what to do next. I felt like I was putting us first.

By asking her to come along, I was offering the best thing for the both of us on this journey. I told her, "You wouldn't have to work if you don't want to, but if you want to, that would be your choice." Once again, I thought it was a good offer.

Karen was quiet for a moment, as she stared at me blankly. It was an uncomfortable silence, and the waves which appeared so serene just a moment ago now felt like they were marking the excruciatingly slow passing of seconds.

Finally, she followed up with a terse response. "If that's what you feel about all we've been through over the last three years, why don't you go to Atlanta and play and after the season's over in seven or eight months, whenever it ends, if you come back to Newport from Atlanta, call me up. If I'm still available, maybe we can go out." This was followed by a longer silence. I was surprised by the anger in her tone because we had a good three-year love affair by that time.

I docked the boat and drove her home. It felt like a long ride back. After I dropped her off, the confusion settled in. I had another decision to make. I knew who I had to go see.

Before the sun was up the following day, I was driving back to UCLA. I knocked on Coach Wooden's office door. He answered right away and welcomed me inside. The familiar sight of his office walls lined with framed signed letters from his former players reassured me that he was the right mentor at this crossroads in my life. He had spent a lifetime instructing these players whose words of gratitude he looked on every day. He had guided so many players through the game but more importantly through life, which was his calling.

I was so full of anticipation that I got right to the point before even sitting down. "Coach, I'm not sure what to do about Karen. I've just signed a three-year contract, and I'm not sure I'm ready to marry her. I mean, she's amazing. We have so much fun. I would like to build a life with her, but I just don't know if I'm ready." It took Coach a second to respond:

"John," he said and pointed across from his desk behind me. I turned around and saw the original Pyramid of Success that he had hung directly opposite his desk.

"I wish I would have put love at the top of this Pyramid."

He went on. "We can give without loving, but we cannot love without giving. In fact, love is nothing if we cannot give it to someone. While you are wondering what you can get out of this relationship, you're missing the most powerful thing about love. Ask yourself what you can give to Karen? A marriage? A life? A family?"

I sat there without words for a few moments. It was another hard conversation and another long silence. He said "John, Nellie Riley is the only girl I've ever loved and the only girl I've ever kissed. We were married for fifty-three years. And after her death, I continued to write her letters and poems once a month and placed them on her pillowcase."

I wondered before responding, "Do I have a love that deep?" I was only twenty-one. I asked, "How can I be sure this is the real thing? How can I be certain?"

He contested my inner doubts with a wise question. "Do you love her?"

I quickly replied, "Yeah I do, Coach, with all my heart."

He asked, "Can you picture a life without her?"

I responded, "We have a good life together, and we are committed."

Coach interrupted me by sticking his index finger into my chest and right into my heart. He looked at me as if he was reading my mind and commanded me, "John, you marry that girl!"

With just five simple words, Coach managed to upend my possible plans of freedom while in Atlanta. At the same time, he gave me the wisdom I sought, and I found myself unable to discount it. I entered that meeting looking for an answer, but instead he coached me with the skills to make my own decision just as he had on the court.

I thanked him and drove back down to Newport Beach and mulled over his words. I called Karen, who agreed to go out with me the following day. We didn't talk about our conversation from the previous night. She had made herself clear, and I knew not to bring it up until I had developed a clear decision. She didn't say so at the time, but I knew she was mad. She wanted more than to just follow me and live together. She wanted to be committed to one another in marriage. I think she would have ended it if she didn't recognize my sincerity. She extended patience and kindness and continued to see me.

My fear was unwarranted. I had committed to so many pursuits in my life that led to success. I committed to the work, the coaches, and the team members at Corona Del Mar, Orange Coast College, and UCLA. I had no aversion committing contractually to an NBA team for three years in a city that I knew a little about. I was certain that making commitments in other arenas was a choice for greatness, and I knew this relationship deserved greatness. The decision was made.

I was prepared for that night except for the ring. Surely she would understand that the money was coming later, right? I went through the proposal in my mind, prepared the speech, got down on a knee, and forgot it all. There I was with no ring and no proper proposal.

All I could mutter was, "Um, so, will you marry me?"

Somehow she said, "Yes!" Of course, Karen's sarcastic style was thrown in as she said, "You mean with a ring and everything?"

I had one more person to talk to. I said to Greg, "You've been my best friend since fourth grade, and there is only one person who I can think of as my best man."

He was excited for me and said, "Can't wait for you to meet my girlfriend Lynn." He followed that up with, "John, you know you gotta bring a ring to this event."

I said, "Great idea, Greg."

When the pastor said, "What God has brought together, let no man separate," I thought to myself, "He got that right because only God could bring me together with a wife as amazing as this."

It wasn't as forceful as Coach, but at the reception I said "Greg, you should marry that girl." He and Lynn have been together ever since.

Chapter 8
PLAYING IN THE REAL WORLD

"At every turn of my life, I understood another element of Coach Wooden's teachings."

*~ **John Vallely***

We left right away for our honeymoon in Hawaii. It was good to find time to get a break from the grind. When we returned, we packed up and moved to Atlanta so I could begin training for the NBA. Living in Atlanta was one of the best things to happen to us. We were isolated and far away from our friends and family. Our honeymoon in Hawaii and now a move to Atlanta gave us plenty of time to build a life together. I was glad to return and focus on the excitement that the draft had created.

Everything that I had learned at UCLA helped me function in the NBA. I had honed my skills in mental preparation, strengthened my character, and understood more about race relations because Coach Wooden gave me the right education and exposure.

The NBA is a business, and your mission in this professional environment is to make a living. While many rookies get sidetracked by the lifestyle, my college life lessons applied quite naturally, especially what I learned about being a team player.

The role of playing as a backup to UCLA guard Walt Hazzard and to "Pistol" Pete Maravich would require even greater sacrifice from me than my time at UCLA. Since his early days in the crib, Maravich had been programmed to be a basketball player by his father, whose name was Press and who would become Pete's coach at LSU after telling him, "If you don't sign with LSU, never come home again."

While my work ethic was relentless, it revolved around surfing and sailing. Pistol Pete's ball handling drills involved dribbling until his fingers bled and trying to maintain his dribble out the car door window as his father drove. Although Maravich became college basketball's all-time leading scorer with a record that stood until Iowa's Caitlin Clark broke it in 2024, Pistol never won a championship.

He was an athletic marvel, but he never learned how to surrender to the team because of his tunnel vision. Unable to make his team better or put himself in the true team context, he could not conjure enough sensitivity to understand the individual worlds from which they came.

Being in the real world allowed me to see through the artificial barriers we established in college. In my first year with the Hawks, we happened to be in Chicago at the same time as UCLA who was playing Loyola, and I dropped by to see how Coach and my former colleagues were doing.

I was excited to spend some time with Sidney, who had been my roommate on the road, and see how he was doing. He was on his way to the Final Four's "Most Outstanding Player" award, The Sporting News "Player of the Year" award, and eventually the NBA "Rookie of the Year" award. I was happy that I could be even a small part of his rise to greatness.

I was glad to see Coach Wooden.

Coach was interested in our lives and became a lifelong mentor to me and many players. He asked, "How is the NBA?" He followed this with, "How is Karen and how is your marriage?" I responded, "The NBA is tough as you've probably seen by my playing time, Coach. But Karen, she's the perfect teammate. Marrying her was the best coaching you ever gave me, Coach." Coach said, "Don't get discouraged about the playing time, John. Give your best, and it will all come together. As for Karen, remember that friendship comes from mutual esteem, respect, and devotion, as well as loyalty to yourself and to all those depending on you and whom you depend upon."

Although I had moved away from so many important relationships such as Coach Wooden, Greg, and my former teammates, the friendships I had formed with them would carry me throughout my life even as physical distances increased. Nevertheless, I was also excited to create a new team.

At every turn of my life, I understood another element of Coach's teachings. I was feeling hopeful to grow my family with Karen, and the team spirit block began to reflect lessons that I would carry with me into my family. As a player, I had experienced team spirit. As a husband, I was now learning what sacrifice meant to my marriage. I had heard Coach Wooden describe it as "a genuine consideration for others, an eagerness to sacrifice personal interests of glory for the welfare of all."

When we respect each other, we earn respect and gain strength. The court I shared with four other brothers wearing the UCLA blue and gold was creating gameday moments, but the court I shared with Karen would be my greatest arena.

My time playing in Atlanta wasn't quite what I had imagined, and I would lean on her for support. The Hawks were loaded with guards, so I never found myself getting the chances to play like I had back at UCLA. On March 20, I broke out for twenty-four points on eleven of eighteen shooting. I thought I had turned the corner until I got the unsettling knock on the hotel door.

The assistant coach banged and shouted through the door, "The coach and the general manager want to see you."

With my average of just 4.1 points per game, I knew what was coming. I had to go home and tell Karen, "We're moving to Houston. Start packing. I've been traded."

At twenty-three years old, we were not worldly by any stretch of the imagination and had to pack up everything and move to a new city again. That was life in the NBA. You ride the roller coaster of life to its end, which always comes sooner than expected. For me, it came after three short seasons and an average of 2.9 points per game. My contract with Houston was not renewed.

We returned to our home in Newport Beach and rented an apartment above the water and enjoyed life by the sea together, which we had both longed for while I was at UCLA. Every day we took a sailboat out and watched the sunset together. These days I reflect back on life in Newport, which are some of the moments that I hold closest in my heart. It was just us, the ocean, and the bright prospect of our future. Yet, all transitional spaces soon give way to something new.

A few months later I was contacted by a pro team in Brussels, Belgium called "The Lions." They had sought Coach Wooden's advice on a coaching decision, and he recommended me as the perfect candidate. They contacted me to see if I had any interest in being a player or coach.

I called Coach Wooden to ask for his advice. He believed that I could be a great coach, but he wanted to know if I could adapt to this role on the sidelines. I signed my contract a few weeks later. We were on the road again, and this time it was in a foreign country.

I was twenty-five years old and had been invited to coach and develop a team in America and take it over to Brussels, Belgium. Coach Wooden had taken a risk in recommending me, and I wasn't going to disappoint him. Some of the players were former NBA players with considerable talent, but now I was involved in the draft and searching for players who would be great team players like the ones Coach Wooden surrounded himself with. As the first day of practice approached, I thought through all the lessons that Coach had given me on my first day in addition to two years of Coach's teachings. I thought about that great lesson from Coach that began our first meeting when he said, "Men, please remove your shoes and socks."

In Belgium, they knew that UCLA had a hugely successful program, but they were not yet aware of the legacy of Coach Wooden. They looked at me like we had looked at Coach Wooden back in 1969 as a little bit corny. We built an excellent team using Coach's teachings. I taught them about success, peace of mind, and love. When we started winning games, the players bought in just as we had bought into Coach Wooden's lessons and began to practice them throughout our lives.

Karen and I were far from the luxury life of the NBA. We had a tiny apartment with a "Murphy Bed" that folded out of the wall. Every night after practice, we dragged the mattress on the floor. All we had in the kitchen were a two burner stove and a mini fridge. To do laundry, we had to drain the washing machine in the kitchen sink, and it was constantly in use. We had this little tabletop washing machine that was about three feet by three feet. Karen washed my uniform every day, and every night after dinner she would wash my uniform in that little washer and hang it to dry overnight on the radiator.

CHAPTER 8

I loved my team in Brussels, and passing on Coach's teachings with a talented team was a dream. Needless to say, I decided when I would go into the game and contribute. About half way through the season, we learned that the league, which was American funded, didn't want to finance it for another year. It didn't matter to us, and we still worked as hard as we could every day.

It was during this time that Karen and I found out that our family was going to grow. One day after practice, I went with Karen to the doctor, who barely spoke English. We knew enough French to confirm that Karen was in fact pregnant. We were both shocked and overjoyed.

We went to Belgium to lengthen my career, and Belgium made me realize I was done with the game. It was rewarding as a coach, but I was unfulfilled as a player who had come from the highest level of collegiate basketball and the NBA. Even so, the basketball letdown was overshadowed by the addition of a child to my "family team" and gave me more motivation than I've ever had as an athlete alone.

So I worked as hard as I could to finish that season strong. Karen wanted to stay in Brussels with me until the end of the season and, concerned that both of our mothers would be yelling at us from across the ocean to get home, we didn't tell anyone that Karen was pregnant. When we came home and Karen was five months pregnant, everyone was a little shocked but thrilled at the prospect of welcoming a baby to the family.

Those days were sweet and romantic, and I understood the magnitude of a love that Coach did not want me to miss. We knew that we were going to head home eventually, so we explored Europe together before this baby changed our lives.

The Gotthard Panorama Express journey took us on a boat trip across Lake Lucerne to Flüelen and a train journey along the historic Gotthard rail line. Together, Karen and I went through the Alps, passing castles, scenic shores, and vineyards to the peak of the 12,900-foot

Bernina mountain range. I watched the many twists and turns of the train through tunnels and over bridges and viaducts from our train cabin window.

To be honest, I wasn't focused on the majesty of Lake Geneva and the Alpines at 11,000 feet. I was mostly captivated by Karen's face, which grew increasingly more beautiful with this child, and her indescribable joy when she placed my hand on her stomach to feel the kicks of our child. I reflected on how foolish I was to consider this uphill life journey without her.

I thought to myself, "What other teachings have I still to learn from this Wizard of Westwood?" As we descended from the 12,000 foot drop, I could feel our child's powerful kicks. Karen said, "His name is going to be Eric." I didn't need to ask any more questions. She had just found the most perfect name for our son.

When the season ended, I was ready to retire from the game. As I thought back to my first day in Coach Wooden's team room and his definition of success written on the hand-out, I knew that I had given my absolute best to the game and to my basketball career. I was also about to give my best to love my family and had a desire to further develop the property on which I had learned to shoot baskets. With Eric's upcoming birth, and ultimately the birth of our darling daughter Erin, these children would alter my heart and my destiny forever.

Chapter 9
ALL IN

"Fifty percent of what I will teach will be the fundamentals of the sport, the other fifty percent of my teaching will be the fundamentals of life, particularly The Pyramid of Success."

~ John Vallely

These early family years were some of the most rewarding of my life, and each day I was filled with excitement from building stronger relationships with Karen and our children. For the next nine years, our lives were fully focused on raising Eric and Erin and building our Newport Ski Business with partner Jeff Jones from the ground up, and I gave it my best.

I looked in my rearview mirror, and it was as if I blinked and Erin and Eric had grown up right before my eyes. They were now eleven and nine years old, and we were on our way to Forest Home Camp with Greg, his wife Lynn, and their son Austin. It was a Christian family camp in a beautiful lakeside mountain location near Big Bear

California. We all got to stay in the most beautiful cabins together as a family located right across from the George family.

Every day was filled with family fun and traditions that we were excited to revisit year after year. Eric was always especially excited to get on the lake and show off the skills that he developed from a life on the water. It was a place where people came to encounter God, experience transformation, and engage the world. I thought about faith and the daily services moved me, but it was the camp games with my kids that I loved most. Greg and I needed the yearly family canoe race, and somehow our kids were dragged into these races.

The camp sports director blew his whistle, and we were off! It was Erin and me versus Greg and Austin. With only a dixie cup to paddle, it was a good way to splash everyone, mostly Greg and the USC T-shirt he was wearing. While I was splashing, Greg and Austin got a quick jump. Erin shouted at me, "C'mon, Dad, move, move, move!" We were off! Karen and Lynn could only laugh at the silliness of these two old men competing like it was a race for the annual UCLA versus USC "Victory Bell Trophy." When Erin and I crossed the finish line first, it felt like a win versus USC at Pauley Pavilion–and time for a "UCLA 8 clap."

"You know what this means," I said as Greg put on my UCLA hat and chanted "1-2-3-4-5-6-7-8 UCLA fight, fight, fight."

He promised, "There will be payback for this, John."

We later had the canoe race awards at the dinner cabin. For Greg and I, it was like the All-Area, All-CIF Team being announced. The camp director announced, "And in a close second place, Team George." We screamed and shouted for the George family and screamed even louder when he announced, "And in first place, the winners of the canoe race and the Forest Home coffee mug award is Team Vallely!"

Greg looked at me with a playful clap and said, "I have seventy-three of those."

The Pyramid Principle

I shot back, "That's seventy-five for me. But who's counting?" It was all in good spirit.

I spent the following days being dragged by Erin into the inner-tube jumps and dives. Erin loved to hang out with her brother, and he would give her new tricks, flips, and dives. She mastered all of them and wanted me to see them as she shouted, "Dad, watch this back flip!" I slowed down that day long enough to look around at this family that I had been blessed with.

I turned to Karen and was amazed with what God had given me, and I thought this would be an amazing time and place to renew our vows. We walked hand in hand to the camp chapel and recommitted ourselves with vows to a life together and a future as teammates. Looking back now, it's no surprise to me that my life flashed before my eyes. I had no time to reflect within my routine. I filled every day to the brim with activities. In addition to our business, I coached a total of twenty-five different teams combined over the years between Eric and Erin.

Eric played baseball, soccer, basketball, and volleyball. There was no question that Eric had my drive, skill, and love for the game. He knew from a young age that he wanted to play at UCLA and worked towards that dream day and night just as I had. Also like me, he loved surfing and spending time at the beach, which was a great way for us to bond as a family.

We spent many weekends packing up the van with blankets, umbrellas, and a picnic basket and drove to the beach as a family. Erin didn't have the same love of surfing, but she loved the water and the chance to be together as a family.

With business partner Jeff Jones, we created a strong team like the basketball teams that I had played on. By combining my love of sports and my understanding of business that I had gained from my father, I was able to continue growing my business space for high-end ski equipment, and I gave myself wholeheartedly to building great business teams and one of the top ski stores in Orange County.

Jeff and I were teammates. We had hundreds of employees over the span of twenty-two years and could not have done it without team spirit. It was a very special store with exceptional customer service.

I was glad that my children enjoyed spending time outdoors together. Erin would tag along behind Eric while they tested out the latest equipment from the shop. Though she was darling and girly, Erin loved to show up in boys beach and athletic wear. She wore whatever was in style just like the boys were wearing such as Quicksilver, Ripcurl, and Stussy. She kept up with them too.

Erin was simply the most sweet and loving child. She was smart beyond her years. She was a model daughter and a really good friend to me from the very start, and Karen often said that Erin and I were inseparable. Erin took after her older brother, who she adored. At the age of six, Erin started playing soccer on the local teams called "The Riptide" and "The Force." Though she could keep up with athletes, her true love was performing. Whether she was on the soccer field, on a stage at school, or in front of her mirrored closet door at home, she was a star.

Give her a microphone, an audience, or a pair of cleats (which were always perfectly tied), and she would put on a show. She had learned that whether it was a sports team or a performing arts ensemble, the Pyramid of Success would still apply. I let her know that it would not be easy, but that the rewards of living out these principles was well worth it.

During my children's early years, I made sure to integrate Coach Wooden's teachings into their everyday lives. More importantly, I tried to model it by example. Even when my life had no connection to basketball as a player, I still found a sense of grounding through Coach Wooden's life lessons.

Eric and Erin went to numerous UCLA basketball games with me over the years and loved to cheer on their father's alma mater. In 1986, we went to the "15 Year Anniversary" of the '70 Championship, and the team was honored at halftime. Erin walked into the arena and ran straight to Coach Wooden's seat. I watched from afar as he invited her to sit by him, and they talked for a few minutes.

I never really knew what he was saying, but knowing Erin and Coach Wooden, Erin asked him questions about the Pyramid. She poured over it like a UCLA basketball legend, and I knew that Coach would go straight to the top and talk about what it would take a nine-year-old to achieve greatness.

Coach would say, "Competition is worthwhile and the games are important, but what is most important is your preparation, being the best you can be, and finding peace of mind through giving your best, along with prayer."

What a gift to have that wisdom from such a young age. Erin returned to our seats with a big smile on her face and said, "Coach knows my name! He believes in me!"

Inspired by Erin's excitement about Coach Wooden's teachings, I learned that I had the power to spread them past my own household. Eric and Erin's youth leagues gave me a platform from which to teach the fundamentals of each particular game, along with the fundamentals of life, to hundreds of children within our community.

I thought the life lessons were equally, if not more, important than the sport skills. I taught them not to think in terms of winning and losing, but I wanted them to find success and peace of mind in their efforts.

At the beginning of every season, I held a mandatory meeting for players and their parents, and I was grateful to stand before my two children as well as their teammates and pass on to them what Coach had given me.

There would be no shoe-tying lessons for this group, but Erin and Eric had it down.

The first day of Erin's practice, I brought the team and the parents together and explained by saying, "Fifty percent of what I will teach will be the fundamentals of the sport. The other fifty percent of my teaching will be the fundamentals of life from the Pyramid of Success, beginning with the definition of success. Success is peace of mind and self-satisfaction in knowing you did your best to become the best you are capable of becoming."

A parent blurted out, "What is that? Is it some sort of new age nonsense, Vallely?"

I shot back, "No, it's wisdom from the greatest coach ever, Coach John Wooden."

He responded, "Just let my kid play, Coach! She's young and wants to have fun."

I shot back, "Yes, she is young, but she shouldn't miss the opportunity to develop life skills."

He continued to contend with me, "What are you some kind of zealot? Just teach soccer, Coach."

I ended it by saying, "Maybe there are other teams where your daughter would be better suited to follow easier principles, but my team will not be one of those."

I called Coach to tell him I was teaching his principles to teams of nine to thirteen year olds, and he agreed that these principles are simple enough that a child could figure them out and be influenced by them.

When I told Coach Wooden I was called a zealot, he replied, "No one ever said that leadership would be easy, John. Remember, it's what you learn after you know it all that counts." I realized there were parts of the Pyramid that I still had to learn, such as faith through prayer.

Chapter 10
MORE TO LIFE

"The Pyramid is about faith."
~ John Vallely

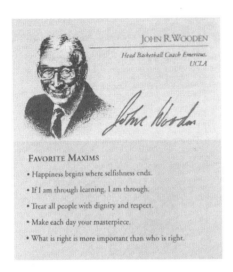

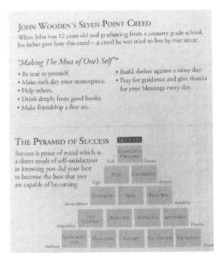

If competitive greatness meant arriving there with faith through prayer, it was clear that I was lacking something. On the surface I seemed to have it all as I entered my thirtieth year. I had a wife and a son and daughter who were the loves of my life. I had a ski shop that was thriving. I had photos and continuing relationships with this community of teammates that won championships together to remind me of what I had accomplished.

My financial investments were sound. My father let me manage the property, with the rising real estate values in Newport Beach. In just a three-year stretch, an appraisal determined the property's worth had increased almost fifty percent. I saw it as an emerging real estate opportunity, so I threw myself wholeheartedly into that as well.

I asked Karen, "Do I seem happy?"

Her response concerned me, which was simply, "No, John."

"Odd, isn't it, Karen? I mean, I've won championships, been drafted in the first round, traveled the world, married the love of my life, and experienced the love of the two children I adore. At the same time, I can't figure out what it is that I'm missing. I feel unfulfilled. This can't be all there is to it with just shooting a ball through a hoop, surfing at sunrise, and winning more trophies." At this point, it was all about getting more money, more real estate, and more accolades.

She said, "John, fulfillment and happiness are different."

I said sarcastically, "Okay, Coach Wooden." This prompted her to respond, "What would Coach tell you, John?"

"He would probably say to give that Bible a shot."

She said, "He's typically right with you, John."

"True, Karen." Then I asked, "Do we still have the copy of his Seven-Point Creed?"

She rumbled through some drawers and found it where it had been collecting dust. I took it with me and went sailing and read through it with new eyes. It was different from hearing it as a player.

1. "Be true to yourself." I knew I was living my ideal life.

2. "Help others." I've coached several teams. That should count.

3. "Make each day your masterpiece." I'm reminded every day that our kids are a work of art.

4. "Drink deeply from good books, especially the Bible." Of course Karen was right. I considered, "Do we even have a Bible?"

5. "Make friendship a fine art." I had the love of friends, teammates and Coach.

The Pyramid Principle

6. "Build a shelter against a rainy day." We've made good investments. At least I thought so.

7. "Pray for guidance, count and give thanks for your blessings every day."

There was "prayer" thrown in again.

I knew we had been rewarded and blessed, and that couldn't have occurred by accident. Watching the birth of our children made me wonder how that could just be a random event, to create a being that thinks on its own, walks, talks, and then grows up into an adult.

I didn't even have an explanation for my own existence. I certainly had nothing to do with when, where, and why I came into the world. I was not put here by my own effort or doing. There had to be something bigger going on. I would have ascribed it to a higher power, except my relationship with God was minimal.

Friends had asked me what I thought about Jesus Christ, but I never took the time to really formulate an answer. I wanted the explanation or the finding without the actual seeking.

On a trip to see some friends in San Diego, I wanted to clear my head and find some answers. I felt weighed down by challenges, and I went to Sunset Cliffs Beach and found a spot on a sandstone cliff that overlooked the panoramic views of the Pacific Ocean on a beautiful day. The waves were turning into soft white foam on the shore, one of the most basic and rhythmic cycles of nature, and I was the only one around to witness it.

As Coach taught me to give thanks for my blessings, I gave thanks for the miracles that I saw that day, including the sun and the wind and my own body, which seemed like its own miracle with fully functioning legs and arms. I could see, hear, speak, and think. I knew I did not make that happen. I didn't do anything at all. I was just there.

I wanted God to reveal Himself to me. I wanted Him to offer concrete proof of His existence and defend His position. I tossed up a casual prayer.

"If You're who You say You are, I'd like to have some of that," I blurted out.

That was it. I didn't promise any dedication or offer of anything on my part. The wind kept blowing and the waves kept crashing. Despite being surrounded by His beauty, power, and glory, I couldn't recognize that some of that was what I was experiencing. This revelation in nature was the very answer.

Truthfully, I wasn't ready to turn over my life. I wasn't willing to open the door to my heart and soul and ask God to be the Coach and the leader of my life. I didn't realize it at the time, but it was immaturity as measured by the level of questions that I was asking an all-encompassing, all-powerful God. Only God could offer a glorious life forever, and the best I could come up with to ask was if I could have some of that glory? It was like asking Coach Wooden on my home visit, "Can you assure me of an All-American career without the work or the coaching?"

I did want the answers. As I stood on the beach that day in San Diego, I was searching for some sort of peace that I was lacking in my life. There was an absence of conflict in my heart. It was the first step of my path towards finding my own peace with God's guidance.

That launched me into a search to satisfy my insatiable hunger. I began to read and investigate the claims of the Bible, as Coach had asked me to do fifteen years earlier. As I had done in any previous undertakings, I went wholeheartedly into my search to find out if He was real. All the while, I remembered Coach talking about faith and finding peace of mind.

I began attending Mariners Church in Irvine, where a pastor had a way of giving sermons that made the stories seem personal and applicable to life. When he said there was a "God-shaped vacuum" in everyone that only God can fill, it sounded like Coach telling us that worldly blessings would not give us the peace of mind we were looking for.

While I expected that integrating God into my life would create an absence of conflict and instability, that was not always true. Although I was getting closer to God, I couldn't say I knew Him. God came to me in the most unexpected of times. One day I was driving home from an investment property I had purchased with a business partner and going over things in my mind. I was having a conversation with myself about these investments and this future. I knew I needed God's guidance, power, presence, and will for my life. I prayed, "Jesus, please come into my life and change me according to Your will. I'm giving myself over to You."

I don't know if I even said the right thing, but this moment was a radical event. The God of the universe heard and answered my prayers. I had given up my spirit and my soul to a God I could not see, but I knew He was real. The peace was indescribable. As I was overwhelmed by the presence of His Spirit, tears were streaming down my face. I had never experienced anything like this before. I think this was the peace of mind that Coach Wooden knew we would find through faith.

I couldn't wait to get home to tell Karen. I said to her, "Karen, I found that missing fulfillment today."

She stared into my eyes, hugged me, and replied, "You look peaceful, John...and happy!"

This was only the beginning, but I was driven by a thirst for more knowledge and a closer connection to God. I committed myself to church. My family came with me, and their lives were changed. I joined a unique team called a men's covenant group that met once a week to read the Bible and pray for each other. This was like athletic training next to Greg, and these men pushed me to grow in my faith.

After years of following the principles of the Pyramid of Success and charting my own course through ups and downs, I realized the unspoken destination that the Pyramid was leading me toward. I went to meet with Coach and shared my discovery. "The Pyramid is about faith, Coach," I said. "The Pyramid led me to God." He could only smile. He knew that the search for competitive greatness would lead us to faith.

He said, "Basketball is of small importance in comparison to the total life we live. There is only one kind of life that truly wins, John, and that is the one that places faith in the hands of the Savior. Until that is done, we are on an aimless course that runs in circles."

His faith was the engine for greatness that inspired him to work, compete, love his players, and teach them to rise towards competitive greatness.

I realized what Coach Wooden taught about peace of mind and God's teachings would manifest themselves with the same results. Peace of mind is the reward that faith can provide.

As Coach Wooden defined it, faith is "belief without evidence." The evidence I had was a peace that I had never experienced. It was a peace that was my tangible proof. I moved forward with trust in the process and believed that something good would come from my effort as had happened on the court. As I understood more of God, I chose to move towards Him because of His presence, which is fulfilling, completes me, and gives me peace in adversity. I was about to find out more about peace in adversity. As I grew, I sought ways to elevate His name, which was different from the life I had lived to make my name great as an athlete.

I thought carefully about what I desired to do with this newfound understanding and prayed a dangerous prayer.

I prayed, "How would You use me and my family for Your purpose?"

Chapter 11

ERIN'S BATTLE BEGINS

"Daddy, pray for me."

*~ **Erin Vallely***

    Eric was an elite three sport athlete, who would follow in my footsteps to UCLA and win a National Championship in volleyball. Erin was athletic, but she was not a natural. She worked hard to develop skills, and she competed in sports to see me erupt in joy when she made a big play or skied a black diamond mountain slope.

Her passion was for performing and visual arts, but she had one mindset which was to give her best to become her best in every arena, especially since I was coaching her team.

On the morning of our tournament soccer match, I approached Erin's bedroom door, which was slightly cracked open, to tell her it was time to get ready. I loved these brief impromptu moments when I could watch this kid perform while she was unaware. She was often singing and sometimes dancing, and her grand jeté leap showed a better vertical jump than mine. At other times she would be painting rainbows on her bedroom wall.

Her life was a creative masterpiece and a work of art. She had learned and followed one of Coach Wooden's favorite practice maxims which stated, "Make each day a masterpiece."

On that day, I heard her beautiful voice singing along to "My Favorite Things"[6] from *The Sound of Music* soundtrack. This precious face with her hair in pigtails was performing with a tutu over her soccer uniform.

"Girls in white dresses with blue satin sashes, snowflakes that stay on my nose and eyelashes, silver white winters that melt into springs, these are a few of my favorite things," she sang.

Erin was dancing and singing with her theatrical free spirit and singing into her hairbrush as a microphone as if it was opening night on Broadway.

"When the dog bites, when the bee stings, when I'm feeling sad, I simply remember my favorite things and then I don't feel so bad," she continued to sing.

I didn't want to interrupt, but after watching for a moment, I knocked and announced, "It's game time, Erin. Are you ready?"

She responded, "Almost, Dad." I watched her smooth out her socks nice and tight and perfectly lace up her soccer cleats from the bottom. "Good and snug," she said as Coach had taught us. Next, as a pregame ritual, this nine year old competitor slapped the poster of "The Pyramid of Success" hanging on her wall next to a watercolor rainbow and shouted, "Let's go" just as I would have in 1970.

Karen and Eric showed up to the field, prepared to cheer as always, and Erin played her heart out. It was down to the final minute, and the score was tied 2-2. Erin ran to receive a throw in. She made a cut, changed direction, and sprinted down the sideline to break free.

Erin received the pass and accelerated towards the goal. She maneuvered down the field through a number of forwards and midfielders, maintaining elite balance.

Erin took her shot on goal just as the one remaining defender tripped her while trying to steal the ball. Erin went down hard. The referee stopped play and pulled out a yellow card. Erin got up slowly and grabbed her side. I yelled, "You need a sub?" Tough as always, she waved me off but used the moment to jog over for some advice.

Nothing could stop her from taking this penalty kick. She looked at me and Eric. Eric said, "Erin, we've done this hundreds of times. Aim for the far end of the post." She knew the move Eric had taught her. She nodded and jogged back toward the field.

I yelled, "Hey, Erin, be quick but don't hurry." She knew the Coach Wooden-ism and smiled.

Erin faced off against the goalkeeper, and her brother started to lead a chant, shouting, "Erin! Erin! Erin!" She approached the ball, stutter stepped, faked the goalie to the right, and blasted the ball into the upper left corner of the net for the score.

Erin's teammates swarmed her in celebration of their victory. Eric ran onto the field with a group from the stands that surrounded this champion. Erin was all smiles that day.

Later that night, I went in to check on her. I stuck my head in her room while she was resting on her bed with an ice pack on.

I went in and noticed that she had displayed the championship trophy below a copy of Coach Wooden's Pyramid of Success that was directly above her. I asked her how she was doing. She responded like a champ and said, "I'll be fine. Probably that hit I took. I'll come back strong."

I said, "That was some fake before the penalty kick."

Erin responded, "Like you and Coach always said, Dad, it's the little things that make the big things happen."

I was proud of that kid. I said, "You know, Erin, I've been waiting for a game like this since you started playing."

She hugged me and replied, "Me too, Coach!"

Erin always played tough and aggressive and liked to attack the ball, oftentimes running through the opposition as she did that day. When the pain started, we thought nothing of it. We assumed the complaints of pain in her leg and stomach were just a result of her fearless style of play. I became concerned when it escalated into four consecutive sleepless nights as a result of the sharp pains in her leg. We massaged it, gave her Tylenol, and waited patiently for it to subside.

On the fifth day, she came into our room and said, "Dad, I really want to practice today, but my stomach is pooched out." Sure enough, it was the size of a cantaloupe. We went quickly to her pediatrician, who referred us to the top pediatric oncologist, Dr. Mitch Cairo.

An MRI and a biopsy a week later led to a diagnosis, and Karen and I returned for the results.

"I'm sorry to tell you that the pathology report revealed a cancer called Rhabdomyosarcoma." We sat close together, and I held Karen in shock as our tears began.

"How is that possible? This kid is in perfect shape?" I questioned.

"We don't know why they get it, John," Dr. Cairo confessed. "What we do know is that this particular type of cancer is most common in children under the age of ten. It typically starts in the soft tissue of the skeletal muscle cells which control all voluntary muscle movements, but it can form anywhere in the body."

"How can this child with amazing physical strength and ability as an athlete and a dancer have an afflicted muscular system?" I asked.

He replied, "Erin's is most concentrated in her bladder."

I breathed to regain my balance and asked, "What's next?"

"I need to schedule an emergency surgery for tomorrow morning," Dr. Cairo said. We were mentally ready the next day, and as Erin rolled towards surgery, Karen and I held her hand.

I said, "Erin, you're tough, you're resilient, and you can beat this."

Karen added, "We love you, Erin, and we're here for you.

Erin responded, "I know, we've got this! Team Vallely."

She was only nine years old, but she had a calm, balance, and peace that reassured us that my little fighter was prepared. Her grip was tight, but her face was peaceful. She whispered faintly, "Daddy, pray for me."

Karen's strong arms that had pulled sailboats carried heavy book bags, carried me all the way to UCLA, and carried this child in her arms were now placed around me as we prayed.

Erin's prayer request made me realize that everything Coach taught me about the Pyramid was moving me towards prayer.

We were concerned that it went long, and they opened her up for five hours of surgery. Dr. Cairo came to the waiting room where Karen and I were praying. I jumped up and said, "How is she, Doc?"

He looked troubled as he sighed, "Erin is okay, but it was the most angry tumor I've seen on the job. We got ninety-seven percent of it, but the other three percent will be treatable…difficult, but treatable."

"What does the treatment involve?" I asked

His response was more than I hoped for as he answered, "Extensive Chemotherapy."

We composed ourselves and went in to see this little fighter.

Karen and I held her hands, and the touch awakened Erin. She was still groggy but smiled as I said, "How you feelin', Erin?"

She whispered, "Wait 'til you see my penalty kick now without this tumor, Daddy."

I felt a wave of relief, only to be followed by the awareness that this was where the real challenge would begin. I looked at my daughter as she rested in the recovery room, with an IV hooked to her chest. My nerves were shot, but I had been conditioned by Coach to compartmentalize my emotions and accept the challenge with assurance.

I hadn't given it a second thought on the basketball court, and now we were talking about my little girl. There was no question we would fight as hard as we could to put this child in the best possible environment.

She was only nine years old, but she was already a student of Coach Wooden's Pyramid. She knew even more than I did that prayer was what she stood on for balance, but this would test my faith and my peace of mind.

Most of the tumor was gone, but what about the 3% that remained of this malignant monster? Would the constancy of my prayers work with chemotherapy? Time and time again, I returned to faith and attempted to "rejoice in hope, be patient in hard times, and pray all the harder."

My time was better spent praying and taking action rather than going down endless spirals of questions to grasp at some semblance of control, which is what Coach would have told me. I could only let this lesson sink in when it came back to me from my nine-year-old daughter, who learned it from Coach Wooden. He was more than just my coach and was now our family's coach through this time.

After Erin was home and stable, we entered her room and knew that the only comfort she had right now was her stuffed animals. Bub was a three-foot tall purple bear to her right, and Smokey was a pound puppy to her left. Smokey wore a hospital wristband and had an IV dripping in his arm that was covered with rainbow bandaids. They were Erin's patient partners in her journey.

As she sat huddled between them with an anxious look in her eyes, I knew I had to go see the man who taught me and my daughter to stand strong in the face of adversity. I went to see Coach Wooden at VIPS Diner on Ventura Boulevard, where he was a longtime regular. We sat at his special spot at table number two, which was right below the photos of Coach, his teams, and his Pyramid of Success.

I thought about my new team Vallely, which was my family. It would give me the hope I needed.

I got right to the point and told him, "Coach, Erin has cancer."

Coach's eyes welled up with tears as he said, "I am so sorry to hear that, John." He quickly regained his composure.

I continued, "I know you gave me the fundamentals of how to compete, but now I'm faced with circumstances beyond my control."

Coach spoke with the confidence of a post practice huddle like it was 1969. "At UCLA, you became a great competitor with preparedness and a foundation. That foundation prepared you to face any test, John."

"Thank you for that, Coach," I said.

CHAPTER 11

The lesson continued.

"That foundation is balance, and that emotional balance is created by the faith that you have found." By this point, I was choking back tears.

"Control everything within your power, John, which includes being the best father and husband you can be. Keep your emotions under control, with good judgment and common sense. With the things you can't control, leave those to God's care."

I then asked Coach the most difficult question and said, "Why does God allow sickness and disease?"

Coach thought for a moment before responding, "I'm not sure why He allows awful things to happen, especially to children, John. There are times when He intervenes and times when He doesn't. God doesn't promise to make all bad events good, but He does promise to make something good out of a bad situation if we love and trust Him."

A life of faith sounded simple and peaceful when Coach said it, and it had a simplicity when Jesus stated, "Let the children come to Me. For the kingdom of heaven belongs to these."

My child Erin understood it. Faith is what gave us balance as my darling daughter would battle through chemotherapy sessions every three weeks for two and a half years. She endured several surgeries and many rounds of chemo every three weeks for two and a half years, with Karen and I switching off to spend nights in the hospital with her.

Erin went to school every day that she was able and to soccer practice to support her teammates. Representing the heart of team spirit, this kid was out there cheering, high-fiving, and keeping stats. Her physical presence reminded her teammates to keep their balance. At home, she had a rolling pole that held all of the chemicals she needed in a bag that dripped into her intravenously, she remained vibrant. That pole was a nightly reality next to her bed while she slept. We called her pole "R2-D2" after the tagalong robot in the movie *Star Wars*.

Erin remained upbeat, did well in school, loved life, and approached every day as a special opportunity. Outside the hospital, we tried to develop normal family routines like watching *The Sound of Music,* which she loved. We were thrilled to see her use her years of theatrical training when she was cast as an extra in the film coincidentally titled *Dying Young.*

Around this time, Coach Wooden came to speak to my seventy-five employees at the Newport Ski Company. He was eighty years old now but still sharp as a tack. Coach spoke as if he was addressing a basketball team in 1969 as he said, "I'm happy to be here because, first and foremost, I am a teacher. I believe teaching may be the most important and rewarding job on earth."

My greatest teacher was my father who would say, "Johnny, remember this and remember it well. Never try to be better than somebody else, but never cease trying to be the best you can be. You have control over that but not the other." Coach also taught me to judge my success based on the quality of my effort rather than how I stacked up to someone else, whether it was on the basketball court or in the classroom or in life.

Coach gave me a poem which has had a tremendous influence on my life. He used to pull out this Van Dyke poem and read it to our team. He now began reciting it to the group of employees.

He said, "Four things a man must do if he would make his life more true, to think without confusion clearly, to love his fellow man sincerely, to act from honest motives purely, to trust in God and heaven securely."

I was watching our employees' faces, and they were locked in. Coach continued, "I know that if Jeff and John hired you, you must be competitive and skilled at your job. Let me leave you with this last thought: Be the best you can be!"

What a moment this was. I know later in life Coach was paid extremely well to speak, so this message from him was a gift.

He came to my office afterwards, and we spoke about life. He asked how Karen was doing and of course how Erin was doing.

I said, "Erin is a fighter, Coach!"

He said, "I know she is."

"But," I continued, "she's sick from the toxins, and the chemo has wreaked havoc on my little girl. The anti-nausea medication isn't effective, so Erin constantly feels sick and often vomits in the middle of the night. Bacteria has weakened her immune system and caused infections, so on top of everything else we have to load her up with antibiotics."

"I'm so sorry, John," he said. His compassionate eyes were tearing up. "How are you doing?"

I told him, "I'm doing everything within my power, Coach. But it's a fierce opponent."

Coach said, "You were always a fighter, John. Keep your balance." He signed a copy of his business card and handed it to me, along with the poem he just read and the 7 Point Creed. Coach said, "Please give this to Erin and tell her I'm praying for her." I stared at it for a moment. It read, "John Wooden, UCLA Head Basketball Coach Emeritus."

Erin was grateful that Coach thought of her, and she seemed to improve. She still had chemotherapy sessions, with all of the side effects that wreaked havoc not only on her system but on her self esteem. She also needed to have several surgeries on her bladder, but she was relentlessly determined to perform in the Christmas concert. On the days she had chemo, she brought her music and practiced while she underwent treatments. She would sing for the nurses at the Children's Hospital, who loved her.

When she was picked for the Christmas concert solo, she ran into our living room when she got home that day and shouted, "Dad, Mom! I was picked for a solo of 'I want a Hippopotamus for Christmas'!"[7] We were thrilled that it gave her a new hope and joy for life.

The sound of Erin practicing and the sight of her dancing in her bedroom gave us joy as well. There were days when she was too weak to stand, but she would never let the illness get in the way of her preparation. On those days, we would see her laying on the floor on pillows while singing in front of her mirror.

After weeks of practicing, the day of the Christmas concert arrived. Karen spent the morning adding the finishing touches to her costume. Eric, who was an ideal big brother and deferred to his sister, helped Erin carry her things to the auditorium. As only a big brother could do, he gave her a pep talk. I watched this from behind the curtain, and his words affirmed a hope that made me teary-eyed.

"I know you've worked hard for this, Erin, and I have heard you prepare for tonight," he said. "I know you're gonna crush this. With or without this performance, I'm always proud to be your brother."

She placed her frail arms around him and said, "Thanks, Eric. I'm so proud to be your sister." She didn't want us to stand backstage with her, but Karen insisted on being there in the wings. Eric and I sat in the audience waiting for her to take center stage.

The spotlight came on, Erin stepped on stage, and the entire audience exploded with applause. The music played, and her face lit up. For a moment under those lights, we all saw Erin as perfect and as the way she had always been. She danced and smiled while singing, "I want a hippopotamus for Christmas. I don't think Santa Claus will mind, do you? He won't have to use our dirty chimney, just bring him through the front door. That's the easy thing to do!"

Halfway through the song a group of her friends shouted, "We love you, Erin!"

"I can see me now on Christmas morning, creeping down the stairs. Oh, what joy and what surprise when I open up my eyes to see my hippo hero standing there! I want a hippopotamus for Christmas. Only a hippopotamus will do. No crocodiles or rhinoceroses, I only like hippopotamuseses, and hippopotamuses like me too," she sang.

When the song finished, Erin's friends rose in a standing ovation. The cheering hit me like the applause at the NCAA Championship Game but with much greater meaning. In the midst of her own battle, she brought an indescribable amount of joy to our family and our whole community.

She walked off stage and into the arms of the other performers who congratulated her. Karen helped Erin lie down until it was time for the final bows.

She appeared exhausted except for her face, which was radiating and brilliant. In the curtain call, the final bows were announced by song. When they brought Erin back out, the crowd's applause was electric as she bowed and smiled.

After the concert, she was too tired to go to the afterparty, and she had another treatment the following morning. She got the chance to share her voice with her loved ones that night, and she had given her best to get there. Coach Wooden's meaning of success had defined her.

We had come back stage, and I watched as that perfect face looked at her mom. Without much energy left, Erin whispered, "Thanks for helping me make it to this day, Mom."

I assumed the duty of watching over Erin, and later after Karen and I had gone to sleep, Erin woke me with shouts of pain. She couldn't stand the suffering anymore. Hearing the agony in my daughter's voice broke my heart and cracked my faith.

In a battle more intense than I had ever imagined, I shouted, "God, where are You? And what are You doing? Why are we here all by ourselves?" I knew He could handle my frustrations and maybe He would respond to my passionate pleas, but I was losing balance with this villain I could not control. I felt helpless in the torture of this child I loved so very much. I poured out my heart to Him. I can't say that I trusted Him at this time, but I knew He was a refuge for Erin.

I can't explain why God allows things to happen this way. Yet, without a sense that God oversees everything that happens, it would be easy to spiral into chaos.

My faith was shaken, but my daughter and her highlighted Bible kept me hanging on by a very strong thread.

I attempted to control the things that I could control, the tangibles and the intense intangibles. As Coach had advised me, I grabbed ahold of that which kept me in balance, which was a trust that God had a plan for me and family. I knew this plan was bigger than I could fathom, and the balance that Coach Wooden taught allowed me to balance my anger with gratefulness, my pain with rejoicing, and the thought of death with the promise of heaven.

Maintaining that perspective allowed me to have some amount of peace, but faith is also making a tangible commitment. That commitment applied to my marriage to Karen just as much as my parental devotion to Erin. Keeping my family together as a team while supporting Erin reflected that our family was as high-functioning as the great teams under Coach Wooden.

Accordingly, we established a game plan. This meant that sometimes Karen and I would spend days and nights apart. Karen would spend nights with Erin, and I would relieve Karen to spend time with Erin during the day. Then in the evening, I would do my best to be home for Eric when he got back from school. He was a highly compassionate kid and loved his sister, but he needed a family.

We met with Dr. Cairo again. When we got to this point, all we wished for was some hope, and he gave it that day in a powerful way as he announced with a sigh of relief, "I'm encouraged that the chemo appears to be shrinking the tumor. We still have to continue the treatments, but it will not be as aggressive so we can focus on rebuilding Erin's strength."

Chapter 12
LAST DANCE

*"You are the most amazing person
I have ever met!" Erin had now
become the coach and the teacher,
and I had become the student.*

~ **John Vallely**

After twelve months of Erin's improving health, we went to Palm Springs on a family getaway to celebrate the end of her treatments. The month before her final chemotherapy treatment, with what seemed to be extremely positive results, Erin appeared re-energized and happy. She was jumping, diving, and catching balls from Eric as she jumped off the diving board.

She was now wearing a wig from the hair loss. One day, unaware that her wig had become loose, she jumped into the pool and the wig popped off. She looked around confused as the kids in the pool started laughing and pointing at her. As Erin saw her wig floating on the water and felt the stares from the other kids, she began crying uncontrollably and ran back to the hotel room. It broke our hearts.

I followed her to the room and tried to console her, but it was a bigger issue than the wig. The frightened look on her face reminded me that she was only eleven, and she was battle weary from enduring this fight.

I said, "Erin, take heart in the fact that with everything you have been through, you were willing to jump in that pool. That is a powerful testament to your strength and character."

She knew I was trying, and she said, "I love you, Daddy."

Not long after the pool incident, she complained about a pain in her abdomen, which we planned to address when we got back in a matter of days. While we were driving home, she felt unbearable pain, so we went straight to the hospital. The tests showed that the tumor had returned.

We had been through two years of therapy with only one treatment to go, and now this villain known as Rhabdomyosarcoma had returned. She was sobbing and said, "Please help me. Isn't there someone who can help me?" The tears were breaking my heart. There was only one place to turn now, and we latched onto faith in Jesus.

Erin was determined to attend the yearly "Father and Daughter Valentine's Dance." We scheduled her treatments around it for her to be in the best shape possible for the big night. Once the night arrived, Erin traded out her regular surf clothes and hospital gowns for the prettiest dress I had ever seen, and we hopped on that Ferry ride to the hundred year old Balboa Pavilion at the water's edge.

As we walked up the steps, Erin was more brilliant than the 1,500 lights that illuminate the Pavilion and the Bay below. She was flashing a big smile and a happy face, which melted my heart because I knew she was dying inside. The smile was slowly fading on her little face under hair that was a wig.

She was getting weaker, and as I held her I could feel that her body was more fragile than I had realized. As we danced, all the people in the room seemed to fade away as I took in this moment with Erin. The future was uncertain, but I was determined to give Erin as much joy as possible. With the sound of Bette Midler's powerful voice filling the room, we danced and swayed like there was no tomorrow. I could hear the lyrics, fully encompassing the moment. "Did I ever tell you you're my hero? 'Cause you are the wind beneath my wings."

Erin looked up at me with that sweet little face and said, "I just wanted to make it to this night."

I looked back at my darling daughter and replied, "This is my greatest night ever."

She said, "Don't let me go, Daddy."

I tried to respond as best I could, and I whispered through my tears as I was fighting the urge to cry, "Never, Sweetheart."

The song ended, and Erin ran over to greet her friends. I quickly exited to the hall to collect myself. I knew I needed to choose the kind of mindset that I would have taken to the court for a championship game. I needed the mentality that I had chosen every time I needed to be at my best to get through a difficult situation. I focused on the aspects of competitive greatness that involve choice. I could choose anger, sadness, or doubt; or I could choose poise, enthusiasm, and initiative to be grateful for what I had in this moment.

I chose to give my absolute best when my daughter called upon me, and I went back in and danced the night away with the most wonderful daughter anyone could ever ask for.

After more than two years of chemotherapy treatments and multiple surgeries, our options—and her time—were running out. She had been so brave along every step of the way, and the last thing she deserved was more discouragement. We went back to Dr. Cairo, who saw no improvement.

The prognosis was that she would need a bone-marrow or a stem cell transplant. It is a tremendous amount of trauma for a little body to endure the impacts of two years of chemotherapy and radiation, but a transplant like this would be beyond daunting.

During our time at the hospital, we had seen several children pass away when the transplant didn't work. Erin asked if she could survive it, but I wondered if any of us could get through a transplant. First, they needed to attempt a different chemotherapy cocktail to get the disease into remission before they could attempt this drastic procedure.

Even at her weakest moments, she brought light and inspiration to the hospital staff and other kids in the care of the pediatric unit. She made cards in the shapes of hearts and rainbows with kind messages for Dr. Cairo and the nurses.

She made one card in the shape of a heart that would stay with me forever. It read:

"GOD IS MY HERO.

Because He is wonderful. He loves me alot.

He is with me wherever I am.

He prays with me all the time.

He gets me well. God is my life.

Without Him I would be very sad.

I love Him."

The first phase of this new radiation portion of her treatment allowed her to remain at home. We considered this a small gift, given that she could be as comfortable as possible and that we could at least feign a normal family life for her sake.

Toward the end of that cycle, she had a bad reaction called hyper-pigmentation, in which her abdomen turned black. Her skin looked like it had been barbecued, and her blood pressure dropped so low that she went into the critical care unit. We didn't know if she was going to make it.

It was during this new round of chemotherapy that she became my hero. She was in the bathroom, bleeding and vomiting, with tears running down her face. I was sitting on a trash can next to my poor little girl, realizing there was not much I could do except hold her and try to cheer her on with hope.

I had run out of Coach Wooden lessons and Bible verses about hope and heaven. I was out of answers as to how she was still holding up and still believing. I was rubbing her teary face softly with a wet towel and my hand. I looked at her face and asked, "How do you do this, Erin? How do you keep fighting?"

She stopped heaving for a moment, gathered her strength and composure, and with confidence responded, "I pray."

I was immediately awestruck at the power of this little human be-ing, and I held her in my arms and marveled. I told her, "You are the most amazing person I've ever met, Erin!"

Erin had now become the coach and the teacher, and I had be-come the student. Erin walked by faith, and not by sight. This level of faith needed my effort and actions. I now saw prayer as an exten-sion of what I could do. It was something I could master and add to my arsenal of hard work and striving. My understanding was that if I prayed hard enough, God would answer; if I put in the work, the results would come.

I assumed that an unanswered prayer was a result of not praying enough or not doing enough work or having enough diligence or intensity. Maybe I did not have enough faith, or maybe I had not spent enough time on my knees. The peace of mind, as Coach taught, was knowing you did your best. In that arena, the answers would come.

Erin found that prayer was waiting, seeking, and listening. It was more than an answer. It was the peace of God. It is certainly challenging to have peace while your daughter is in unending pain. I was struggling to find it, but she did.

It was through God's presence that we were able to find peaceful moments. As we read her Bible together and she highlighted verses, I found the promises about heaven to be the most comforting. I added some of her highlighted verses to my understanding, including a verse from Philippians, which was written while its author was chained to a prison guard and awaiting death, with an uncertain future.

"Don't worry about anything, but pray about everything. Tell God what you need and thank Him for all He has done. Then you will experience God's peace, which exceeds anything we can understand."

In one of Erin's favorite verses in John, Jesus says, "I tell you for certain that everyone who hears My word and believes in Him who sent Me, has eternal life and will not be judged, but has passed out of death into life (John 5:24 paraphrased)." Another verse reads, "I love the Lord because He hears my voice and answers me. Because He bends down and listens, I will pray as long as I breathe (Psalms 116:1-2 paraphrased)." My little warrior was teaching me faith from God's perspective, and I wanted to find that faith.

Erin's remaining days were uncertain, but we wanted to make life as easy as we could and give Erin things that would bring her joy. She always wanted a baby miniature pig, so against my better judgment we went and got her a pig.

The introduction between Erin and the pig made it worthwhile. Erin screeched, "You got me a pig!" She hugged me and Karen and then hugged the pig and blurted out, "Oh, Porky, you are so cute!"

I teased, "Its name is Porky?"

"Yeah, Dad. You don't like it?"

"Only because Daffy Duck beats up Porky," I replied. It was a cute pet, and from the moment she placed Porky in her arms, that little pig loved Erin like she was sent from heaven.

The love and happiness this cute and cuddly pig was able to bring her was what she needed. Porky would let Erin hold her for hours. Unfortunately, Porky hated me. She not only made a mess in the house, but she would bark at me in defiance. Yet, the second Erin came around, Porky was back to her docile sweet self. Porky gave Erin around-the-clock affection like a puppy, which made us glad as Erin weakened and was spending more time sleeping with Porky next to her.

Erin grew aware that her time was running short, but she was no less confident of her purpose. When given the chance to speak at a black tie Pediatric Cancer Research Foundation Gala, she welcomed the opportunity. Karen dressed her up, and she was beautiful again that night. They were both beautiful, and Erin's spirit was beautiful.

An audience of 400 donors, friends, and supporters of pediatric cancer research looked on in awe when I called her onto the stage. I stayed close, ready to help her through this. She waved me off and said, "You can sit down, Dad. I've got this." With confidence and clarity, she gave a speech that has affected the lives of hundreds of thousands of pediatric cancer patients.

She said, "Thank you all for coming out this evening and also for your support of the Pediatric Cancer Research Foundation. I want to thank Dr. Cairo and all the doctors, nurses, and staff that give me such wonderful care."

The audience applauded and Erin took a deep breath to continue. "Unfortunately, there is also an enemy here with us. It is an enemy to all of us including men, women, and especially children. That enemy is cancer, and it is an enemy that must be defeated!"

Once again, the audience applauded as she persevered. "There is really only one way we can defeat our enemy," she said. "And that is through research. Research will give us the weapons we need to win every battle!"

I don't know how she held it together because I certainly wasn't. I'm not sure there was one dry eye in the room. As she finished, she clarified the anthem that would be the foundation of her legacy by saying, "I'm asking you, please continue to give! Please continue your support, and together we will see victory against cancer!"

The entire audience stood up and gave a standing ovation to my daughter. With confidence and toughness, Erin provided an example of courage for many of us to follow. I would need to follow her day-to-day example of maintaining balance, faith, and hope. Going forward, I would look back at her courage as she faced not only surgeries but the thought of death itself.

It started to dawn on us that the end was coming, even if we weren't comfortable talking about it. One day, as we drove home from the hospital, Erin asked, "Daddy, will I live until Christmas?"

I was now operating on fumes, and that question overwhelmed me. I had answers for everything but not this question. I remarked, "I don't know if I'm going to live until Christmas, Erin, and no one gets to know how long they're going to live. But my prayer is that we both get to have Christmas together."

She replied with an even tougher question, "Daddy, why do I have to die?"

With the heaviest heart a father could have, I evaded the question at hand and addressed the answer with the truth of heaven. There's no comforting response when your daughter asks you why she's dying, but at least I could offer that I firmly believed in a heaven where there is no pain or agony and nothing but joy in our hearts and our existence.

"This I know, Erin. If you don't live until Christmas, you will be in heaven, and it will be perfect. And you can hang onto the hope that God will wipe every tear from your eyes. There will be no death or mourning or crying or pain, for all these will be gone forever."

She turned towards me with a look of anticipation on her face as I continued, "It's a place where there's no chemo, no radiation, and no suffering. You will feel love from God like you can't imagine because God is crazy about you, Erin. And one day you and I will be in heaven, and we will live forever together."

"I can't wait, Daddy." She added, "He's crazy about you too."

That is what we grabbed onto in her last few weeks. Without faith and hope, there would be nothing but chaos, anger, and disappointment. When I think that the greatest coach in basketball history led me to that understanding, I'm in awe of my journey.

Erin had encountered and believed in a real Jesus, and her hope was real. There was hope in her healing. If not in this life, she had hope in a perfect healing in heaven. Even more so, she had hope that her life was still part of a perfect plan. As that Bible was highlighted, "I know the plans I have for you, declares the Lord, plans to take care of you, plans to give you the future you hope for. When you call on Me and come pray to Me, I will listen. When you come looking for Me you will find Me."

One of Erin's favorite songs was "In This Very Room," and it was playing in her room as she neared the end.

> "In this very room, there's quite enough love for all of
> us, there's quite enough joy for all of us
> there's quite enough hope,
> and there's quite enough power, to chase away any
> gloom;

for Jesus, Lord Jesus, is in this very room."[8]

Erin gave us hope, but I quietly wondered why a sweet eleven year old girl who sang and believed in His power could not receive a powerful healing on earth. I was still angry yet balanced as Coach had taught me in a defensive stance.

Without that balance, the accumulation of negative thoughts would have overwhelmed me. I had faith in God, and I had peace that I put forth my best effort to be the best father and friend to Erin that I could be.

It was my greatest application of the Pyramid of Success, knowing I did everything that was humanly possible to deal with her illness.

Coach Wooden never set victory as a goal. With Erin knocking at death's door, I could finally see the wisdom in that thought process most certainly as it relates to life. Victory was impossible in this case. The doctors told us that Erin would not survive. Though the sorrow was unbearable, as any parent in our situation could imagine, I realized that one triumph was that we managed to keep our family strong. We would continue to do so even without our darling daughter. I felt that strength with Karen, as we stood by Erin's bedside while she was in and out of a coma near the end.

Erin suddenly came out of a coma, opened her eyes, and clearly asked me, "Dad, what kind of wine do you like?" I was surprised and shocked. I thought it was Erin's answered prayer! This was her healing! I held Karen's hand, and we looked at each other in disbelief.

With encouragement, I answered, "Erin, I'm glad to hear your voice."

Erin repeated the question again. "What kind of wine, Daddy?"

I exclaimed, "Red wine, Erin! Cabernet Sauvignon."

She closed her eyes, and those would be the last words she spoke. That question would not make sense for many years, until I would go through another battle.

The end came in the middle of the night, with Karen and I sitting by Erin's bedside in the hospital room. Her breathing was slowing down. Karen and I were holding Erin as she took her last breath and passed on to eternal life in heaven. We sat in silence with disbelief and wept.

At that moment, it felt as if everything had been stripped away. I didn't want to accept that I couldn't change this outcome or that there was nothing more we could do. I never envisioned that it would end this way. Even in Erin's case, where a doctor warned us that no more could be done and we had time to prepare, it still challenged my emotion and intellect in a way that was simply too much for my brain to process.

I consoled myself with the thought that she was in heaven, and I truly believe that she is. Yet, it didn't ease the pain. Karen and I gathered Erin's belongings from the hospital one last time. We eventually went out to tell the nurse that our daughter had died. The doctor, nurses, family members, and friends all came to the room at dawn to say goodbye, and we thanked them for their help and all they had done for Erin.

We returned to our home, now vacant of our daughter, and felt empty of hope. We placed Bub and Smokey on her bed. These two stuffed animals had comforted her for every hospital trip until the very end, and we sat on her bed and broke down and cried. Karen's voice was trembling as she said, "John, we have to make final arrangements for our daughter's memorial."

The planning of Erin's service and the impact of the loss penetrated my soul with a severity that was beyond comprehension. I was distant and angry, and I was aware that I was devoid of compassion and love for Karen and Eric.

I finally lost it with Porky. That pig was peeing all over the floor, messing up the carpet, and aggressively barking at me. What was once a member of our team to support Erin had now become a nuisance. Pigs are intelligent and have emotions, and Porky likely sensed that Erin was gone. She seemed to be squealing almost from loneliness. Karen saw Porky as an extension of Erin and had an affection for her. She picked her up and said, "I miss Erin too, Porky."

Karen and I disagreed about keeping this animal because I couldn't take its noise and behavior anymore. I snapped at Karen, "It's either me or this pig!"

She looked at me, looked at the pig, and then she picked up the pig and said, "Let's go, Porky" and walked out the door.

I knew that a high percentage of marriages end in divorce after the death of a child, and I was concerned. Karen was going through her own grieving, and I should have been more sensitive. I now had to confront the uncertainty of my future as I managed the grief alone. We were both devastated by Erin's death. This had nothing to do with the pig, but the pig forced the breaking point.

Karen went to Palm Springs for a day, which gave us both time to think. My thinking was cloudy, and I spent the time in bed and stared at the ceiling.

I had to guard my thoughts and senses and think of the eternal and the unseen, where faith resides. I needed to focus on what I knew to be true in faith and hold on to the promises of God even while life was falling apart.

I also knew I had to return to Coach Wooden's thoughts on team spirit. The stakes here were clearly much higher. I had made huge sacrifices as a captain on my senior UCLA team, and now I needed to sacrifice for the benefit of Team Vallely. This would be the greatest test of my ability as a team captain.

I could now relate to the greatest loss ever suffered by the coaching world's greatest winner. I went to see Coach Wooden at his home. Coach understood my devastation.

"The thought of life without Erin hurts so much, Coach," I said.

"I know it does, John. I felt the same way after Nell died."

I asked, "Do you ever move past it, Coach?"

"At the time, John, I didn't see the sense in going forward. Nothing seemed the same, not even basketball. I even stopped attending the Final Four weekend, which we had always taken together, as the thought of attending without her was too painful."

"I understand that, Coach. I can't even walk past her bedroom," I said.

"You can see it in this home, John. I have kept all of Nell's possessions exactly as she had left them." We sat in silence as I glanced around the living room at the possessions and the volumes of books which Coach had accumulated. I looked back at his eyes, which spoke volumes of sadness.

"When I advised you to marry Karen," he said, "I told you that I continued to write Nell letters and poems, placing them on her pillow on the twenty-first day of every month, the date of her death."

"You did tell me that, Coach, and it changed my view of sacrifice."

"Come look at this stack, John," he said. "It is now two hundred and four letters. I miss her every day."

"How do you get back to peace, Coach?"

His sad eyes took on the joy that I saw at the Championship net cutting in 1970.

"It's only the thought of being with Nell again eternally that sustains me and removes my fear of death, John," he said.

I knew Coach would bring me back to faith. Then, as if we were at practice years ago, he began talking about the 7 Point Creed as if it was the first time. Coach advised me about gratitude. His strong voice that had instructed me at center court of Pauley Pavilion all those years ago was teaching me again.

He said, "John, it may help you to look at the blessings instead of the disappointments." His voice trembled, as he continued, "Look at all of the good that came from Erin's life."

I nodded and said, "You're right, Coach. We were fortunate for those short years we had Erin with us, and in that short time she managed to make Karen and I better. And even more, she gave us unimaginable joy."

On my way out, I saw a wedding day photo of me and Karen. It was as if Coach had placed it there on purpose.

"Karen loves that photo you have of us, Coach," I said.

"You know I love Karen," he responded.

"I know, Coach, she loves you too."

And that made me realize that I needed Karen to return, with or without Porky. I made a call to Eric, who said she was already on her way back. When she pulled into the driveway, I met her at the car door and said, "I missed you so much. If you came back with a pig, an elephant, or a giraffe, I'd be happy."

I was relieved when Karen stepped out of her car without the pig and sobbed, "I missed you too. I already returned Porky to the breeder."

I pulled her in close, and we both cried.

Chapter 13

A SIGN OF GOD'S FAITHFULNESS

"Somewhere over the rainbow way up high, and the dreams that you dreamed of once in a lullaby; somewhere over the rainbow bluebirds fly, and the dreams that you dreamed of really come true."

~ Israel Kamakawiwo'ole

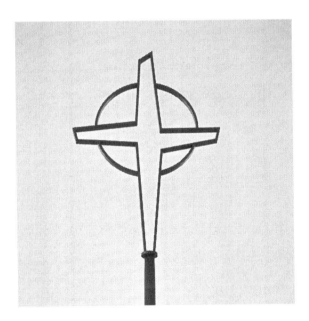

Throughout Erin's battle with cancer, I struggled to grasp how such a sweet little girl could be put through this ordeal of spending painful nights in hospitals instead of carefree days in the schoolyard with her friends. In the time that has passed, I have found clarification that began soon after Erin died when we held a memorial service. 900 people showed up at Saint Andrews Presbyterian Church to honor the impact of this powerful little life. Nurses, doctors, teachers, friends, and their families, as well as kids from the community and around Orange County had heard her story and were moved by the magnitude of Erin's strength and courage in the face of adversity.

I was amazed by the dramatic impact our little girl had on her community. Her impact continues even decades after she passed away as people who are facing life challenges are encouraged by the details of Erin's battle and the mindset that accompanied it.

At St. Andrews Presbyterian, I knew I had to speak but didn't know if I could hold it together. As we sang the song "Amazing Grace," I reflected on the words as this local choir of 900 of Erin's friends and their families sang. It was like heaven came down to that Newport Beach Church.

> When we've been there ten thousand years,
>
> Bright shining as the sun,
>
> We've no less days to sing God's praise
>
> Than when we first begun.[9]

It was comforting to consider that Erin was in a place that was so beautiful and magnificent that praise was all around! The citizens of heaven who had been there for thousands of years were in awe and still praising.

Erin's favorite place was the water, and the times we spent there as a family made the ocean a logical place to honor her and spread her ashes.

On the day of her burial at sea, there was a torrential downpour, and the forecast indicated that the storm would not clear for hours.

Erin loved to paint rainbows, including the ones she had paint-ed on the walls of her bedroom. For that reason, we played Israel Ka-makawiwo'ole's ukulele version of "Over the Rainbow" as the yacht moved slowly out of the pier.

I began to mouth the beautiful words, "Somewhere over the rain-bow way up high, and the dreams that you dreamed of once in a lul-laby; somewhere over the rainbow bluebirds fly, and the dreams that you dreamed of really come true. Someday I'll wish upon a star and wake up where the clouds are far behind me, where trouble melts like lemon drops high above the chimney tops. That's where you'll find me."

The ocean was turbulent and so was my soul, as I held Erin's ashes in one hand and grasped onto Karen's hand with the other. I couldn't let go. I let the song play, and I reflected on all the dreams I had for her life. I already longed for the day when the dreams of heaven would really come true for me.

I was brought back to this moment as Karen pointed to the sky. No one who was not there that day would believe what happened next as the dark sky began to clear. It was as if God had peeled this image off of Erin's bedroom art wall and pasted it up in the sky, where a rainbow appeared directly in our path. I wanted so badly to keep going towards that rainbow, but we had a drop spot for Erin's ashes. The boat slowed as we arrived at the coordinates. I held on and held on, and Eric stepped towards me with tears in his eyes and put his arm around me. He took the ashes from me. We all said goodbye to Erin and let her ashes go.

That rainbow was a sure sign of God's faithfulness. Since that day, at critical times of life when I need a sign or an encouragement, God splashes Erin's rainbow across the sky. With each rainbow, we know and feel her presence as well as His.

I don't know why God allowed Erin to pass away, and I don't know why God allowed us to suffer. Yet, I do know this: He has used it to help many others. That knowledge of life at its very core, which can only be learned from the most trying of challenges, is valuable and costly.

I asked myself, "What should I do with this knowledge?" I have come to understand that whether you live twelve short years as Erin did or for almost a century like Coach Wooden, all of our journeys are brief. The main thing is how we live those years and learn, share, and respond while we are in the process. That is what determines how fulfilling the journey can be.

Despite the knowledge that Erin was at peace, it was no less painful. We tried to stay upbeat, but it was hard to take pleasure in life. Karen and I went to Hawaii with friends, but the joy was absent from the trip.

Karen thought of our honeymoon and how brilliant the skies were. She remarked, "These sunsets are set in black and white."

We returned to a similar mood at home in Newport Beach as we continued to grieve.

Three months after Erin passed away, she came to me in a vivid dream. In the dream, I was in a room with Karen as we waited to see Erin's oncologist. While we were seated, I looked to my left and Erin walked in through a side door, stood there, and smiled at us. She was perfect and looked as if our prettiest picture of her had suddenly become animated with vitality and personality. Her voice was inaudible to me in this dream, but I received her message as she stared at me with a look that told me, "Everything's okay, Dad. Get on with your life."

It was so pleasant and peaceful at that moment that it gave me hope and closure. The dream of Erin in perfection started to make sense. It was not perfect sense, and it will never make perfect sense on this side of heaven, but I can't wait to join her in the amazing heaven that she finds herself in now. Erin's life may have been cut short, but it was dynamic and special. I know that she's carrying that zeal with her for eternity in heaven. I felt it so strongly in the dream.

When I woke up, I realized that I still had purpose in this world. I had my fantastic wife and my terrific son Eric, who needed me. With a renewed passion for the game, I decided to help coach Eric's high school basketball team, where he had become a sharp-shooting guard at Newport Harbor High School. The time together was a welcome return to our old routine, as Eric's life had taken a backseat during Erin's illness.

As a basketball family, we had spent countless hours in the alley playing one-on-one and H-O-R-S-E. It was during this time that Eric reminded us that we were still a family: Team Vallely. He came to me one morning when I was at my lowest and said, "Yes, we have lost one of our team members, but we must still rely on one another and God. Dad, we are still a family. Don't dwell on what we don't have, but rather dwell on what we do have. We have each other."

Although I could still imagine my sweet daughter in pigtails, with her perfectly tied high tops and making bank shots, this return to the court with my son was exactly the distraction I needed from the grief.

The Pyramid Principle

BATTLE WITH A BANKING BEHEMOTH

"Are you right?"

~ Coach John Wooden

My dreams were about to become a nightmare, and I suddenly found myself in a legal battle for the land that I had begun to help my father with. For a moment, I was up against a tall defender with outreached arms again. Yet regardless of the mismatch, I knew I had the tools. I dribbled into the lane, and this time I was ready. I was also wiser and pump-faked so the defender jumped past me. I passed the ball to the cutter because I understood the role of the team. Now I would need a team with me to battle against the "Banking Giant" known as Bank of America over the bayfront property my father bought in 1935.

Based on the Life of John Vallely

In Downtown Los Angeles, the Bank of America Tower stands as a monument to power and is highly visible at the top of Bunker Hill. From 5th Street, it's a steep climb uphill, with 101 stairs to the entrance. This banking behemoth towers over the city at 735 feet and fifty-five stories. It was constructed strategically so the four sides face a true north, south, east, and west. My legal case was going uphill and sideways, and everything was caving in until Harry Carmack stepped in.

I was referred to Harry Carmack, who was a no-frills, no-nonsense lawyer and went to visit him in Costa Mesa.

Considering I was a junior college player that was overlooked and still picked to start for Coach Wooden, I was happy to find an underdog legal team to take on Bank of America. At this point, the law firm's name and size didn't matter, but I was surprised that he was a one-man team in a small office. He kept the drapes closed in his office so he could concentrate on his work. I was waiting for a personal assistant at the front desk when he came out and greeted me.

Harry said, " Hi, John. I was a big fan of your days at UCLA."

I replied, "Thanks, Harry! I heard that you are a knockdown shooter in the courtroom."

He responded, "I do my best," and I knew he was the right guy.

I told him, "When I started handling our family's business property on the Balboa Peninsula, I had no idea that I would be the underdog in a legal drama that put our home and financial foundation on the line. And it seems like something suspicious is going on as the Bank of America has tried to sidestep its way out of more than six decades and millions of dollars in lease payments."

Harry understood and said, "I already know the game they're playing, John. How many boxes of filings have their big money lawyers produced for you?"

I groaned, "Start with a stack of seven phone book-sized volumes of deposition transcripts, next to eighteen inches worth of motions, filings, and memos. There are boxes filling my attic."

Harry asked, "How far are you willing to go, and would you take a settlement?"

"No way, Harry," I shot back. "We already turned down a settlement offer of half a million dollars."

Harry said, "This will test you, John."

I replied, "A worthy opponent brings out the best in me, Harry."

"Even if they cheat, John?"

I answered, "God gives us talent and gifts, Harry. One of mine is my competitive drive. I won't be intimidated by the opposition's money and influence."

I told him the story:

The strip of waterfront property on the Balboa Peninsula that became the basis for my fight with the Bank of America represented seven decades of my family history. The property in question was my father's land, which included the Bay View Hotel and its pier and prime location by the ferry boat landing. Plus two 30-by-60 foot lots on the corner of Edgewater and Palm.

The hotel wasn't a grand resort but commanded a prime view of a 180-degree vista spanning from Bay Island and Harbor Island on the left spanning to the harbor entrance on the right. The rolling Corona del Mar hills served as a backdrop, while commercial boats and luxury yachts passed each other in the foreground. On a clear winter day, one could see the snow-capped peak of Mt. Baldy in the distance.

Soon after he bought the Bay View Hotel, my father had the opportunity to buy the four adjoining lots. It was undeveloped land except for a small snack stand on the corner, but it was a perfect space for boat repairs and limited parking.

After I retired from basketball, I wanted to help my father with the changing real estate market. It was time for our family to adapt by retiring the old business and capitalizing on the new economic possibilities. Dad said, "We'll never make money in real estate." Then he started getting these checks from the property that were much better than what he was making when he was working his tail off.

Harry responded, "UCLA Econ grad, right?"

Sure enough, Harry had done his homework. I nodded and said, "Bachelor's degree from UCLA, Masters Degree from Wooden."

The saga continued, and I told him how I had wanted to improve our cash flow from the property without incurring debt. The most attractive option was a seventy-five year ground lease. It carried lower risk for us, while allowing anyone who leased the property a chance to improve the property at their own cost.

Harry interrupted, "Smart move. Any default by them could not be held against you."

"I thought so, Harry."

In 1988, a developer held the lease and chose Bank of America to finance the construction of his new project. At the time, we were filled with optimism and high expectations. It seemed like our investment was about to take off. This would be the first step towards what eventually became a court battle between me and the bank. He sub-leased the space to a restaurant, a few small shops, a fast food establishment, a marina, and a four-level parking garage. It was the garage that proved to be the undoing of the entire deal.

Harry reasoned, "So, the garage never generated the revenue it was supposed to bring in?"

"Correct, Harry, and due to the language of the ground lease, my family was not on the hook for this shortcoming."

Harry was listening, as he poured through a law manual.

"With the loan and interest up to almost eight million dollars, the developer was beginning to sink under the weight of his investment," I explained. "He and his company couldn't keep up. It declared bankruptcy in 1989."

Harry was skilled in bankruptcy and understood. He said, "That should have been the cue for Bank of America to foreclose on the construction loan. Then the bank could follow normal procedure, sell its interest, and assign its position in the Vallely Ground Lease to a third party."

I continued, "Right! But Bank of America didn't want to follow the standard procedure or be held responsible for the fees in liens against the building for money due to subcontractors."

Harry shot back, "The bank thought it had a quick way out."

"Right again, counselor," I sighed.

Harry said, "Give me a few days and let me see what I find out." I already admired Harry's initiative and resourcefulness.

I went to our property after that meeting and thought of my days as a kid when I would help my dad with a rake and a wire scrub brush. The joy and pride I felt doing a great job for my dad was far more important than the money he paid me. It was a strong reminder that this land was sacred to our family and was worth fighting for. The stakes were high in both sentimental and monetary value.

Harry called me back a few days later with what he discovered.

"I went to the County Recorder's Office and saw that in April of 1989 the bank directed its subsidiary, Bancamerica Commercial Corporation, to buy the assets of Balboa Landing. They took over the loan financed by the lending arm of the bank and agreed to all of the terms of the Ground Lease. Then the Bank of America attorneys assigned the ground lease to BACC, indemnifying the principal holders of Balboa Landing from any further obligations."

Harry continued, "Were you ever never notified as required by the terms of the original ground lease, John?"

"Never," I responded, with my heart beating out of my chest.

Harry's voice grew more animated as he announced, "Then by assuming ownership of the title in this rigged transaction, the bank was legally obligated for the lease for sixty-two years."

I shared Harry's excitement but countered, "Yes, but Bank of America didn't intend to stick around for even sixty-two months. They expected another lease assignee to buy their position or, if any assignee did not pay rent, we would file an unlawful detainer action that would terminate the responsibility of all parties, including Bank of America. That way the bank would be off the hook for the five hundred grand owed to the subcontractors."

Harry declared, "An unlawful detainer filed against the developer would be the normal course of action, John."

"You're spot on, Harry! One law firm even advised us to take this action when the rent was not paid. Everyone else told us, 'You don't want to take on the Bank of America.' Maybe they were right." I continued, "The bank tried increasingly devious tactics. In 1996, we received a notice of foreclosure on two parcels of land that we owned. That was a shock considering we never had borrowed any money against that property."

The bank used a law firm to write illegal false grant deeds on property that our family owned. In July of 1994, the bank sold our property deeds, and the bank's interest in the Vallely Ground Lease to Edgewater Place, Inc. Now the Bank of America was out of its obligations for the remaining fifty years of lease payments.

Harry said, "Wait a minute, John. I want to be clear about this. Was Edgewater paying rent?"

"No," I affirmed. "They fell behind on the rent, and in May of 1996 the payments stopped coming all together."

We went to court to get a quiet title action on the parcels as a move to eliminate any other parties' interest in our property then decided to sue Edgewater, which then filed for bankruptcy. Edgewater abandoned the project and instead trained its sights on the Bank of America and sued them for wrongful sale. Harry filed an unlawful detainer, and we threw the entity out.

That essentially terminated the lease, and we retook possession of the property in August of 1998. Now that Harry's discovery was big, he suggested, "John, you can also sue Bancamerica Commercial Corporation for the rent due on the balance of the lease terms since they are listed on the lease."

My doubtful thoughts started chiming in, "You can't beat them. Your opponent is the second largest bank in the United States and is represented by one of the biggest law firms in California!"

In my mind, it was almost like hearing a voice saying, "You can't play at UCLA because you're too slow." For a moment, I felt like that five foot three inch, one hundred pound kid again facing another big obstacle.

Regardless of what my family had said to discourage me from continuing this battle, Coach Wooden told me on that opening day of my senior season to prepare for a great battle. With that in mind, I returned to Harry's office.

"I'm ready for a great battle, Harry!" I announced.

Harry replied, "Respect all, fear none."

Bank of America asked for a meeting, and we all met in one of their big conference rooms. It felt like the transition from Orange

Coast College to Pauley Pavilion, with our little team versus their huge corporate structure. They were more polished, bigger, and stronger. I was the slow, skinny, guard in that room, but I had been there before.

They made a substantial offer to terminate the litigation. They backed it up with some legal muscle-flexing, and one of their young cocky attorneys with a smug look cautioned me by saying, "I like you, John. You're a good guy with a moral compass and integrity. And you won some games at UCLA. But if you don't accept this offer, the bank will do everything in its power to win this case. And let me be clear. We'll crush you, John! So please take the money."

I turned to Harry and said, "We're finished here."

The cocky lawyer taunted, "Good luck!" with a smirk on his face.

I shot back, "No luck needed, son. It's all preparation."

We walked down the hall. The offices were quite impressive and far from Harry's one room office in Costa Mesa, but I believed in Harry as Coach had believed in me.

We were quiet for a moment. "It's a simple case, isn't it, Harry?"

Harry agreed, "Yes, there are documents at the Orange County Recorder's Office that show the bank's acquisition of the property and liability for the ground lease. That is the only document that should have mattered."

It took thousands more pieces of paper just to enforce it.

It began with three days of depositions from me to the bank lawyers. I tried to keep my answers as minimal as possible with a yes or no to avoid falling into the legal trap I knew they were trying to spring for me.

The day of the court case arrived.

Harry said, "The lawyer games are about to begin with the briefs and motions and every other volley back and forth between the two sides."

The bank presented a five-part counter argument to our case that cited at least seventeen case precedents. Harry asked them to reconsider, which prompted even more rounds of briefs from both sides. Before the judge made a ruling, Harry called me and said, "John, the bank and its lawyers, in their arrogant manner, have offered to settle the case again but this time for much less than their initial proposal."

I mumbled, "What's the amount?"

Harry theorized, "This lesser amount is probably equal to the amount the bank would have to spend on legal fees for an appeal if the judge ruled against them."

I asked, "What's their play?"

"I think the bank is fishing to see if you have lost your resolve after two years of legal pounding."

I scoffed, "No, Harry. Let's go!"

We were back to court, where Judge Robert Monarch issued his second ruling. He ruled in favor of the bank again and announced, "The foreclosure has terminated the obligations of all the parties, including the relationships by assignment that occurred prior in time."

It was another victory for the bank and another incorrect ruling. After almost three years of legal briefings and difficult-to-understand rulings by the judge, I began to feel a heavy burden of guilt that I was taking my family over a cliff. The judge had stated in a settlement conference that I was being unreasonable, but his ruling made no sense.

I blew off some steam, went to pray, and came back and asked Harry, "What's next, counselor?"

He looked at me with disappointment, and I knew how he felt. Harry had battled and given his best. "The only legal recourse now is to appeal," he sighed. "I want to recommend a skilled appellate attorney." That made me realize that he wasn't trying to extract more fees from me, but Harry counseled, "The deeper you draw in, the higher the stakes, John."

I asked, "What are we looking at, Harry?"

His response was sobering. "If you lose the appeal, you are looking at the legal fees, and the bank would want to be reimbursed for its lawyer expenditures as well. After the first two rounds, you are already in for almost five hundred grand, which is their fair claim because they won. The appeals process would probably be at least another two hundred grand, meaning that if you lose, you would owe Bank of America almost three quarters of a million dollars."

I grumbled, "That's in addition to the money we'd owe our lawyers?"

He responded, "Yes." Then his competitive side came out as he said, "But you still have this legal document that states the Bank of America is on the hook for this lease!"

"That's right, Harry, thank you!" I shouted enthusiastically. I became hopeful again and returned to the beach where I would often pray.

I prayed, "God, You know my path, and I want to trust You. But I'm scared. What would we do next? Where would we live next? I have a family that needs me, and this isn't a pick-up basketball game."

As I listened, He took away my fears and reminded me that He was more than I needed. The verse in Deuteronomy that my covenant prayer group had given me came to my mind. It says, "Pursue justice and justice alone so that you will live and possess the land that the Lord your God is giving you."

I thought of the conditioning I had done on that beach and the lessons Coach taught me at UCLA. Harry had quoted, "Respect every opponent, but fear none."

I respected that the bank would try to squash me, but I had gotten over the fear. My sister and her husband, however, were still nervous. They decided to vacate their share in the lawsuit. Her husband had worked for Ford Motor Company, and he had been on the other side and seen the little guys take on the big guys and lose every time.

My brother in law said, "John, if anyone could win this, it would be you. But no one can beat Bank of America. You've already lost twice in the lower court." I was empathetic to their concerns and knew we were hemorrhaging money.

I went to UCLA that week to remember where I came from. I walked the campus but mostly past Pauley Pavilion and then up "The Janss Steps" at the entrance of UCLA, which counted eighty-seven steps up the climb to campus. I knew I had run and conditioned on those eighty-seven steps, and the 101 steps downtown didn't look so tall. I was mentally prepared for this bank climb.

One of the lessons I learned in fighting cancer is that you have to be prepared to absorb the setbacks and then continue to move forward. You can't think in terms of absolute victory. That's not always obtainable. You can find small areas of competition and win little victories every day. You can't completely triumph over life. You just try to compete and make your best effort as often as possible with peace of mind. As Coach had instructed, "There are many things that are essential to arriving at true peace of mind, and one of the most important is faith, which cannot be acquired without prayer."

I continued to pray and believe, and I went to see Coach Wooden at VIP's Diner. It was always good to sit in that booth below that team photo, especially now. It was a powerful reminder that I had beaten the odds.

I arrived early so I could dream of those days again. Coach came in, and it was always great to see him. He never needed small talk and knew I was there for advice.

"Coach, we lost in the lower court, but I still believe the contract made the bank responsible."

He said, "A contract is a contract."

We both paused for a second. I knew the contract was legitimate, but I still didn't know what to do. He tilted his head down so I could see his eyes unobscured by his glasses, and he looked me right in the eyes.

"Are you right?" he asked.

"Yes, I believe I am, Coach," I answered.

He nodded, looked at me, pushed his glasses back up over his nose, and said, "Then not even a powerful bank and its legion of lawyers should knock you off the base of your convictions, even if it appears that our legal system joined the bank against you."

"Thanks, Coach, that was all I needed to hear."

He pointed at the 1969-70 team photo. "You already have what you need to succeed, John." I left the diner and realized I was also once a "player without."

There is a mortar that holds all the blocks of the Pyramid together. That "integrity mortar" mattered to me and to Coach. It had become a lost term in the sports and business arenas, but I believed that it could reward those who built their lives upon it.

I was pretty much down to the members of my household. I was conflicted but remained confident. I knew that I needed to consult with my son Eric, who would also be affected by my decision. Eric sensed the burden I was under and wanted to help because the stress was consuming me. I was short of patience, and my family felt it. Eric and I needed a day together, and we went out surfing.

The swell period was long, and we had a lot of time on our surfboards to talk.

"Eric, the ground lease represents a large portion of our family's business. I don't want to gamble with our livelihood."

"I trust you, Dad."

"This is your inheritance too, Eric."

"Thanks, Dad, but you worked hard for this family."

"Thanks, Eric. I've always admired your work and dedication. You're a bright kid, and I'm glad you got your Mom's GPA, not mine."

He smiled. "Got your toughness and competitive spirit though, Dad."

"I'm proud of that, Eric."

"Appreciate that, Dad."

"Eric, our house will be on the line to finance the legal fees."

"The documents make it clear that we are right, Dad."

"I agree, son."

" As you always say, Dad, let's go!"

"Thanks, Eric. Let's go indeed!"

We caught a peak, and it was cool to ride side by side with my amazing son.

Later that day, I went for a long walk with Karen, who began saving money for her sailboat at fifteen years old. She would be the voice of reason against my gambler spirit.

CHAPTER 14

I said, "We have a good hand, Karen. Should we play it and live this life as full as we can like we always have? Or should we walk away?"

Karen said, "If we stop now, we might minimize the losses, but quitting now will mean a giant step backwards."

I appealed, "We wouldn't be reimbursed for our legal fees to date, and we wouldn't have income from the ground lease. But we would be responsible for the cost of the property update, and we'd have to find a new tenant."

"How much are we up to now, John?" Karen inquired.

"Millions of dollars," I estimated.

"John, we would be back to square one and starting over at forty-eight years old," Karen assessed.

"If we proceed with the appeal and win, we will get the legal fees back, and the bank will be responsible for rent for the next fifty years."

"What would our little fighter Erin do, Karen?" I wondered.

We thought back to the battle she had been through. She had tried her best, and she did it with gusto.

"I think she would want to know that her Dad had played his hand," I added.

Karen's response was the heart of team spirit as always. She concluded, "I'm all in, John. We've fought many battles together, from getting into UCLA and then the NBA to fighting for the life of our daughter. And at the end of the day if we did lose everything, we have already lived on the mattress on the floor once before in Belgium, and I loved every minute of it."

"Me too, Karen," I declared.

Then Karen assured me, "We're unstoppable together, John! Let's fight this as a team."

That's exactly what we did! We chose Robin Meadow, the appellate specialist attorney, who Harry recommended to represent us for our next round. Meadow did his best to inform us of the high degree of risk associated with such an appeal.

"There is no guarantee of success," he counseled me. "And you could lose."

"We already won," I contended, "when we gave our best."

Our appeals case wound up in the hands of a panel of five judges in the California Court of Appeals 4th Appellate District, Division 3.

In a ruling that came down on April 26, 2001, the judge rejected the five premises set forth by Bank of America and reversed the earlier ruling. The seventeen-page opinion that accompanied the ruling kept coming back to the central point we had argued all along which was, "Since BACC assumed the lease, foreclosure did not extinguish its contractual obligations to Vallely."

I looked at Robin and said, "What just happened?"

Robin Meadow shouted, "John, we won!"

It was such a simple statement yet so profound. It was over. We had taken on the Bank of America, and we won in what became a landmark case certified for publication.

I held Karen close and said, "Thanks for battling with me, Karen."

"Not even Bank of America can stop team Vallely," she announced.

The Bank of America attorney walked past me with his smug face. I had a number of responses ready in my mind including, "Never lie, never cheat, never steal" or "You should prepare better next time!"

I knew Coach Wooden would tell me to keep my emotional balance, and I looked at this underachiever and his weak legal team and realized he didn't know what he was up against! That lawyer thought he was competing against a surf rat who "won a few games."

He didn't realize he was up against a five foot three inch shooter who fought his way to UCLA. He didn't realize he was battling a student of John Wooden who taught him how to make game day adjustments. He had no idea that he was in a court battle with a wife who towed sailboats around Newport Beach by hand. He certainly didn't understand that he was up against a father whose little fighter Erin taught him to battle to the finish with all he had.

I was filled with relief, excitement, and happiness that the system had actually worked. Ultimately, I achieved self-satisfaction and a peace of mind. There was no way to quantify the emotional toll my fight with the Bank of America exacted on me and my family in the wake of Erin's death.

They would have to pay millions of dollars in fees, interest, unpaid rent, taxes, and building maintenance, while continuing to pay the lease. I was grateful to Robin Meadow and Harry Carmack for their relentless efforts. I called Harry and told him we won. I said, "I know you didn't get credit for the win, but your help was foundational."

He was truly excited for me and quoted Coach Wooden saying, "John, it's amazing how much can be accomplished when no one cares who gets the credit."

I called Coach and thanked him for his wisdom, which was a continuing resource that I would rely on repeatedly for even greater battles that lay ahead. Coach never liked the word "winning," but this win was not like beating USC in a game. This win was a monumental victory with our livelihood on the line.

Chapter 15

A FIGHT FOR MY LIFE BEGINS

"I really had two choices. I could find my own competitive greatness, or I could flounder around in chaos, with no hope."

~ John Vallely

Now that we had defeated the Bank of America, Karen and I decided that we would battle and defeat pediatric cancer next. I realized that if Erin's life could have such a powerful impact on our community, I might be able to impact the cure if I joined the fight. I joined the board of The Pediatric Cancer Research Foundation and soon became the President. Coach Wooden's thoughts on team spirit continued to motivate me. His principles were defined by a willingness to sacrifice personal interest and glory for the welfare of all, and I knew that my hustle was meant for more than championships at UCLA. I wanted to defeat this villain that had taken Erin's precious life.

It felt rewarding to raise money and bring awareness to this cause, and Karen and I were thrilled to be a part of a successful fundraising campaign for the new Children's Research Laboratory at Columbia University. We went to New York for the grand opening. As we dressed for the Pediatric Cancer Research Foundation black tie event, I looked at Karen in her black formal dress. She was radiant and as beautiful as she was on our wedding day. I put my arms around her, and I was grateful she had stayed with me through so much. I told her, "You are more beautiful today than the day I married you."

I knew that I looked older from the wear and tear of life's stress, and I certainly felt it. She was kind as she replied, "You look as handsome as ever, John."

The last thing I ever expected to encounter as I got dressed for the event was cancer attacking my own body. As I put on my tie, I noticed a strange bump on my neck. I had always had bad skin from all the way back in my acne-filled teenage years. This swelling felt different. This didn't seem as if it would go away with a little skincare, but I wouldn't let this concern ruin the night. After arriving at the event, I was glad to see the familiar face of Erin's oncologist Dr. Mitch Cairo.

After we caught up on our lives, I thought it would be wise to ask one of the best cancer specialists in the country about the lump on my neck. He asked me a few questions about possible symptoms and had some concerns with my response. He said, "Early detection screenings are always advisable. I'll introduce you to a doctor in New York."

We set an appointment for Monday, which led to a CT scan and a biopsy. The report came back, and the cells were cancerous. It needed more analysis. We sent the pathology report to hospitals around the country including Massachusetts General, Stanford, and the Mayo Clinic for confirmation.

While we waited for the results, my thoughts centered on Karen, Eric, and Erin. I owed it to Karen to give it my all and put up the best possible fight. We had been together since we were eighteen years old and been through so much together. She was the best thing that ever happened to me. She provided everything a mother should to our children and had endured all the trials and tribulations of our lives with grace and resilience.

There are times in life when you want to just move on to the next life, but I couldn't let Karen down. After my little fighter Erin had fought so valiantly for two and a half years and set the standard in the Vallely family, I could do no less. I had my answers. The only thing I could control was my attitude, and I would be the best patient possible.

As an athlete, you're always prepared for adjustments and obstacles, but this diagnosis was more than I was prepared for. I had contracted Non-Hodgkin's lymphoma. How could this be? We had already been through a two and half year battle against cancer with Erin, and we were only a year out from our horrendous legal battle with Bank of America. This would be a different kind of battle because it would be a fight for my own life.

I went for a walk on the beach to sort things out in my head. I went to my usual spot down by the Newport Pier and down toward 17th Street. It was the first of several walks I would make while I pondered my options.

My world had become almost surreal once again. While I was trying to raise money and awareness for children's cancer research, the disease seemed more distant and abstract. I had been surrounded by so much positivity and people who were caring and generous, which was a reminder of the best of humanity and the promise of science.

Now I was faced with the other side and experiencing the agony of the diagnosis firsthand and the fear that my daughter had faced.

As I walked along the beach, the ocean seemed so beautiful and perfect. This was the place where I had sailed at sunset with Karen and surfed with Eric and Erin and trained to make it to UCLA. Yet inside of me, there was a demon in my bloodstream that was attacking my own cells.

I tried to rely on my faith, but I was confronted with the limits of my humanity, which included fear. It was normal and understandable, but I felt as if I had no control all over again.

Once again, I pondered God's role in this. While I turned to Him through Erin's dying days and entrusted Him to care for her after she took her last breath, I was struggling to find His presence for this new challenge. The pain of Erin dying in our arms was still agonizing, and now I was faced with the thought that her fate and short life might be my story as well. I fell down on my knees in the sand and, as I had done before with Erin, I tried to surrender my life, my will, and my health to God's will.

As with every challenge, I had two choices. I could tap into my own competitive greatness, or I could flounder around in chaos with no hope.

Karen reminded me, "Coach always said that a worthy opponent brings out the best in you, John." She was right. Coach Wooden often spoke about the love of a hard battle. He didn't want easy victories against outmatched opponents. It was the hardest battles that enabled his teachings to be proven. In these battles, he could discover if he had truly prepared his players to conquer every obstacle.

This particular battle was not something that anyone would welcome, but I could use the foundation and all of the fundamentals I had built up to that point in my life. I had applied these principles in lesser circumstances, and now it was time to execute them in the ultimate challenge. The reality is that there are no guarantees in life, and we all will face death at some point.

I could see myself in that blue and gold uniform again as I heard Coach's voice like it was 1969. He would say, "People with fight can't get up any higher for an important game because they get up for every game. When they step onto the floor, they always give everything they have to give, whether it's for practice, a scrimmage, or a championship game."

Now I would find out how good my best was when the stakes were life and death for my own survival.

Karen added, "Let's go at it like our little fighter did with prayer." So Karen and I prayed and prayed relentlessly.

The weird thing was that I felt fine physically. Then the night sweats started. I would wake up at all hours of the night, soaking wet, just wanting to feel God's presence in the middle of this fight.

The treatment plan would involve chemotherapy. I was given a treatment program of six rounds of chemo in cycles that were three weeks apart. Each round consisted of a cocktail of several drugs including Cytoxan, Adriamycin, and Vincristine.

I would have two to three weeks to recover followed by another round. The chemotherapy begins to wear down your desire to fight because it wipes out all of your healthy cells along with the cancerous ones. On top of that, severe nausea causes vomiting. Chunks of hair fall from the scalp, and there is cognitive impairment and memory dysfunction, which adds to the ever worsening delirium. We kept Dr. Cairo on my treatment team. He liked the results, although he recommended two more rounds of chemotherapy including Rituxan, which is a cancer-fighting drug that works by bonding to and killing cancer cells.

Another biopsy was taken. We waited for the results, and I prayed and waited with trust. The waiting did not come easy for an old athlete who had grown accustomed to crashing through his obstacles, with his own strength and hard work. This time I would focus on God's strength to lead me through the journey. The more I learned to be quiet, the more I heard His voice. Through His word, He was saying, "Be still and know that I am God."

It concerned me that the results needed more time. I prepared for the worst, but I felt at peace when the sweet sound of Dr. Cairo's voice announced, "The tests show no visible signs of the disease, John."

I was declared in remission. Nonetheless, Dr. Cairo decided to invest in a type of insurance in case the Lymphoma returned. We went to Cedars Sinai to harvest five million stem cells from my bloodstream by drawing blood and running it through a cell separator to squeeze out all of the stem cells. The stem cells were examined to make sure they were cancer-free. No cancer was found. The cells went into frozen storage. In the event that I ever needed a stem cell transplant in the future, we would already have a perfectly compatible donor: me.

I figured I was done with this phase of my life. I returned to a normal routine of the ordinary yet joyful roles of parenting, working, and trying to be a better husband to my amazing wife. I felt renewed and was soaring through this second half of life in prime condition, surfing, and skiing. I was sailing with Karen and falling in love with that song leader all over again. I felt like I was twenty-one.

Chapter 16
FORMIDABLE OPPONENT

"Because of what I learned at UCLA, I had the basis for my counterattack. I had the framework for success that I could adapt to any scenario."

~ John Vallely

I had been getting complete blood counts as a normal follow up to detect if this thief was still trying to take my lifeforce. I was anxious when my team of doctors called a meeting, and I could sense by the somber mood that this was not going to be a bill of clean health. They gathered around me, and Dr. Cairo broke the silence by saying, "The lymphoma has returned."

Yet, what I heard him say was, "The death merchant is back and coming for you again."

I had learned to trust Dr. Cairo, so off the cuff I asked him, "Is there any chance I get to sail through this with some chemo again, Doc?" That would have been a preferable option.

I had learned to read Dr. Cairo's face from all those meetings with Erin and me and knew this was the face of concern as he explained, "If you don't get this transplant, John, it's not likely you will survive past twelve months."

I said, "Doc, this is like a coach telling a team at halftime, 'You're down by forty points. If you score thirty straight points, you'll only be down by 10.'" I could tell that they didn't like my analogy. The truth was that if I came through the ordeal, I wasn't guaranteed a victory but just the chance to keep fighting.

It seemed like all of the ideas lacked faith, but it's not up to the doctors. Every person is different, and they wouldn't be doing their jobs if they told me it was easy. No one is cut out for this. There's no training for it. There's no pre-season when it comes to facing cancer.

I thought back to that practice in 1969, and I could feel Coach Wooden's push as I stood in my stance. I could almost hear the words come from his mouth saying, "Never get too high, never get too low." I knew these years and battles had strengthened my balance physically, mentally, and emotionally.

I said, "Let's go! Tell me what I have to do, and I will take it one day at a time." Like Erin, I couldn't control the disease. I couldn't control the treatment. I would have liked to have said to the doctors, "Load me up, and let's get this done quickly." However, they have very specific dosages administered to patients at very specific times for a very specific duration. I couldn't call a timeout and resume this battle later. I needed a tangible approach to dealing with this challenge.

I had that approach. It was hope. From what I had learned from Coach Wooden at UCLA, I had the basis for my counterattack and the framework for success that I could adapt to any scenario. I was more prepared mentally and spiritually for this event. I would pray harder. I would be more enthusiastic. I would be more loyal to my own spirit of wanting to survive. As in my playing days at UCLA, I wanted to be the best teammate I could be to the many doctors, nurses, and physician's assistants who would invest in me.

While I wanted to win, winning was no longer my focus. I set my sights even higher. I had to find peace of mind about my effort, which was the only thing I could control. Anything beyond peace of mind was just a by-product. The results would take care of themselves and ultimately be in God's hands. Again, I turned to Erin's example, which had faith at its foundation. As I thought back to her hope and her strength when she told me, "I pray, Daddy," those words ran through my thoughts. I considered this an opportunity to feel His presence.

I had my plan of attack. With Dr. Cairo's advice, we decided that the Hutchinson Cancer Center in Seattle would be the best place for the Autologous stem cell transplant. The hospital was right on the water. I felt like I could have sailed my sail boat to the front door of the medical center. I should have been there sailing or skiing on Mt. Rainier, but instead I arrived to fight for my life.

This would be my comeback.

There's a little bit of assistance, concession, and unselfishness in everything we accomplish. No one gets anywhere in life alone. From an act as simple as making a layup versus USC to a task as complex as overcoming cancer, victory only happens with a dedicated group. From the doctors who are literally poking, cutting, and stitching me up to the friends and family sending their thoughts and prayers, these are the greatest team players you hope to find.

I received a number of phone calls from UCLA teammates, who have remained like brothers, including Henry Bibby. He had played on the 1970 team, and he called me from his office where he was coaching at the USC. Henry always made me laugh.

"I'm thinking about you," he said.

I responded, "That's real nice of you, Henry".

He said, "No, I'm not calling out of goodwill; I'm calling to tell you I'm looking at a picture from our playing days on my wall. I'm wide open, but you're dribbling and you're not even looking at me."

I said, "That's 'cause I was a better shooter." Henry laughed, and he also agreed.

"I don't know how a Bruin can wear that cardinal and gold, but if I can just stay alive, I'll even come cheer you on in those colors," I joked.

Henry responded, "I know you'll beat this, John! And I'll have a nice USC shirt waiting for you. By the way, John, you had some big games against Washington and Washington State. This is just another contest for you to shine."

I appreciated all those teammates over the years. Maybe I didn't always do the best job of sharing the ball, but all of my guys knew that if they ever needed me I would be there for them in the same way so many of them supported me when I was sick. There's a bond that's formed in the long hours in the gym, on the plane, or in the locker room that never disappears. Whenever we got together for a ceremony or a reunion, that brotherhood felt like we would tip off that night and score on a quick three on two. Coach was right about love, and the love we had was special.

I needed to hear from those brothers before I went into isolation for radiation therapy. It was such a toxic treatment that no one else could be in the room with me. Just from the look of that lead container, you know whatever is in there can't be good. They opened it up and gave me a radioactive antibody designed to attach itself to the cancer cells and kill them off. It was just me, a Bible, a John Grisham book, and some music. Karen had to sit outside until the radiation levels weren't threatening.

In isolation, I just wanted to die. I felt lonely, lost, and in a mental fog. I looked at myself in the bathroom mirror, and I couldn't even recognize my image. As I stared in stillness, I noticed the humming of the hospital fan, and it took me back to the sound of the ocean wind when I sought God on that San Diego bluff. I reasoned that maybe I should seek Him wholeheartedly again. I thought of Erin's hospital song "In This Very Room," and for a moment I felt peace. I knew that God was still there, He was still in control, and He still loved me.

I was still discouraged at the journey I had ahead of me, but I knew I wasn't alone. There were many people praying for me as I was struggling in isolation for thirty days and delirious from medication.

I tried to recall that I had been through thirty-day intensive training camps as an athlete and was used to pain, but on the other side of that pain was a season, a game, or a championship that I could look forward to. The thing that gave me endurance was the outpouring of prayers from friends and fans of UCLA basketball. These were the same fans who had cheered me on before and were cheering for me again now.

I moved into the chemotherapy room for the next stage. This was three days of a high-dose mix that was incredibly intimidating and frightening. A few days after the treatment began, I started to get mouth sores, which is one of the common side effects, and my mouth felt like a bloody pulp. When attendants examined the sores, I noticed them cringing at the sight. I couldn't eat. I could only consume a mix of nutrient-filled fluids. My kidneys were filtering an endless stream of toxins from my body. They rigged me up to a morphine dispenser and gave me a button to press whenever the pain in my mouth or the toxins became too much to bear. I pumped that morphine into my body so much that I was getting delirious and loopy. I felt that I didn't have control of my senses.

When it was darkest, I would imagine beautiful places as my escape, and it transported me far away. In the claustrophobic tubes they used for the PET scans, I imagined myself surfing in Hanalei Bay, the crown jewel of the North Shore in Kauai, where I had surfed with Eric. I could see the swaying palm trees, feel the bright blue water and gentle breeze offshore, and see Eric smile as he rode that wave into the shore. Other times I would distract myself by returning in my mind to an ice cream date with Karen at Will Wright's Ice Cream Parlor in Newport Beach, where even imagining the taste of the vanilla ice cream in my mouth soothed the pain of the sores.

When my blood cell count was reduced to virtually nothing, it was time for the transplant. The Hutchinson Center staff felt like teammates. I made an instant connection with Dr. Robert Hickman, the doctor who inserted a catheter in my chest to carry the blood. He actually created the device he was using on me. He said, "I'm going to put this line in you, and it's going to be perfect. You have nothing to worry about." It was as though my medical team had added a player like Kareem whose screens always got me open or Henry Bibby whose assists would be right to my shooting pocket.

Coach Wooden had taught us to always acknowledge our teammates with a quick nod or a point in their direction when they helped us out with an assist or a screen. No matter what state I was in at the hospital, even when the drugs had me feeling loopy, I tried to express my gratitude. No game was ever too big for me to point to the guy who threw the pass, nor was any situation ever too drastic to pause to say thanks for a big assist in the Hutchinson arena.

Dr. Hickman gave me great confidence at that moment. I gave him a nod and said, "Thank you for your care today. You gave me hope to survive."

My old stem cells were reintroduced to my body, and they went about their way in my bloodstream. Within fifteen to twenty-five days, the stem cells would begin producing red and white cells and platelets. While my immune system was regenerating, I tried to get up and walk whenever I could. I felt fatigued, but I kept walking and fought back. As I slowly walked to the eastern side of the hospital at 5:30 in the morning, I looked out to see the sun coming up over the 14,000 foot peak of Mt. Rainier, which was aglow in orange, purple, and blue. I couldn't go outside to experience it, and I wondered if I would ever be able to experience such glorious displays of nature again. Yet, I was grateful for this one day and this moment, as some transplant patients were doing worse than me. Some didn't make it.

As I would walk, I felt like Coach Wooden pacing the practice court and sharing his wisdom. I would encourage everyone who passed me in the hospital hall by saying, "Make today a masterpiece" just as Coach would have told them.

I knew that I had something special that not every patient had. I had Karen, the unequaled teammate and Coach, by my bedside. She was there around the clock in the first few days after the transplant, and she was there for all the nights back in the hotel room after I felt a little better. My most essential and fundamental human relationship was accounted for, even if all I could do was hold her hand. I couldn't even talk at first because the mouth sores hurt so bad, but her inspiration and presence helped me battle through this.

I told her, "Every day I'm more thankful that I married you, Karen."

She responded, "Every day I'm so grateful Coach made you marry me."

I was always glad for her sense of humor in moments like these. The hotel became my personal measuring meter. I would walk two or three times a day and track my progress by what room number I could reach. One day it was room 117. Later, the goal was room 199. There were some days that I couldn't do it at all. When I was able to keep pushing and moving forward, I did. While I was in recovery, I searched for anything that would allow me to improve and get to the next stage. I thought of beach workouts with Greg George, pre-season conditioning at UCLA with Coach, and practicing with Ron Von Hagen for the Manhattan Beach Open. The mindset of moving towards competitive greatness and success would carry me once more, along with "faith through prayer."

My prayers sounded like, "Help me improve. Walk with me, God." I realized He was with me and met me in the stillness of my soul. I began to see His answers.

After three and a half weeks inside, they let me go outside. One week after that, they released me from the hospital, but I still wasn't free to go home. They had to be sure my vulnerable immune system wouldn't have trouble warding off an infection.

My blood cell counts continued to rise, and I was strong enough to fight off disease. With the help of antibiotics, I finally got to go home and couldn't wait!

It had been a snowy winter in Seattle and one of the coldest in years. When we took off towards home, there was snow on the road. The weather was so extreme that there was doubt whether we could even make it to Portland. I told Karen, "If this disease hasn't stopped me, the weather certainly won't. We're going home!"

It didn't matter that the roads were accumulating snow and that icicles were forming and falling off the bridge over the Columbia River. There were cars pulled off to the side and others that had slid off into a ditch, but I couldn't wait to get home. We did the 1,100 mile trip in two days.

There was only one song needed on this ride, and we sang it together as if we were twenty-one years old and newly in love. Marvin Gaye always made life magical again. Karen and I sang the lyrics like it was 1970, "'Cause, baby, there ain't no mountain high enough, ain't no valley low enough, ain't no river wide enough to keep me from getting to you!"

As fast as we put the Hutchinson Center behind us, I still had time on the way back home to think about my time there. I considered my conversations with God, and I thanked Him for getting me through and for all of the people who had done so much for this journey.

As we neared our house, we came over the hill in Newport Beach just before sunset and went straight to Balboa Beach. After four months in Seattle and two days of driving, we just sat and looked over the ocean. I took Karen's hand, and it felt like the very first time we held hands and watched a sunset together as freshmen at Orange Coast College.

As the golden rays of the setting sun cast a warm glow upon us, I tried to forget about the heartaches and considered that our journey had been marked by many triumphs as well. I never took our marriage for granted, but this was like being in love all over again. As we watched the sun disappear behind the offshore island of Catalina, it felt like an arrival into paradise.

When you're facing the severity of the termination of your life, every affirmation of your survival is invigorating. I thought about all that we had achieved and accomplished, and I couldn't wait to get on with our life together. I would be returning to my friends and my community and getting another chance to be with them. I was ecstatic. I had come from nothing and from being stuck in a room all by myself to now seeing this vista with someone I cared about so much. I could hear the waves, and I could once again enjoy the beauty of the world. This was what I wanted to live for.

I was struck by the simplicity of it all. The moment was overwhelming. For once, there were no challenges and no obstacles. I felt a tremendous sense of achievement.

My effort to live helped me, but it was granted by a power greater than me. I was alive thanks to medical science and the grace of God. I didn't know why I was given this chance. A lot of people who were in the same hospital didn't get to see the sunset at the end of the day. My journey to the brink of death and back was nothing less than miraculous. I was elated that I had survived the difficult transplant experience in Seattle, and the farther away I got from that experience, the more confident I felt about moving on with my life.

Karen and I traveled to Italy in July and went to Alaska in August. We had a new appreciation for just how precious our time together was and how brief it could possibly be. Italy and Alaska were two destinations that had always captured our imagination. Now we turned them into our reality, with two journeys that celebrated all we had achieved and come through together. I was reminded of that wonderful season of life traveling through Europe as newlyweds.

Deep inside my mind, I still felt vulnerable. I still lived with daily reminders of my ordeal. I couldn't feel my feet because of a neuropathy that developed as a side effect from the chemotherapy. The entire process had shown that my body was susceptible to a disease that could take me to the brink of death, but I remained optimistic. My mind was occupied with thoughts of what would come next. In the midst of all that anticipation came another heavy dose of bad news. My blood was tested regularly to monitor my progress and ensure I remained in the clear. A couple of scans had shown abnormal lymph nodes. They gave the results to Dr. Cairo.

Chapter 17

REMATCH WITH LYMPHOMA

"One of Coach's favorite sayings was 'Move! Move! Move!' He meant it both physically and mentally."

~ John Vallely

A biopsy at St. Joseph's Hospital in Orange County showed the lymphoma had returned. Karen and I went to see Dr. Cairo, who continued to help me manage my ongoing cancer case. Dr. Cairo was a loyal teammate, and we trusted his guidance and knew that my file was always with him wherever he traveled in the world. He explained, "John, this time you will need an unrelated donor transplant, with a more powerful immune system than your own."

CHAPTER 17

I asked, "What are the odds of finding a match?"

His response was realistic as he said, "The odds are low." The truth is that it was really closer to impossible. With the odds against me, I didn't quite know where to turn. The past was too dark, the present was in upheaval, and the future was more uncertain than ever. Karen and I had maintained our balance after we lost Erin. The lawsuit victory against the Bank of America ensured that we could carry on financially. What we wanted more than anything was to have time together without stress, sickness, and the threat of death. We no longer knew if we could attain that. I knew I needed to speak to someone other than Karen and share my doubts so as not to discourage her.

I called Greg George, and I asked him to meet me to surf. I figured it might be the last time, and I met him at our favorite spot called Blackies Beach. This stretch of beach is located just north of the Newport Pier, where every surfer in town would be jockeying for waves. That day it was the perfect combination of swell, wind, and tide that created excellent A-frames with the sun's rays showing through the clear blue water as a spotlight on your ride. They were conditions we could only hope for, but I just couldn't ride like I had in the old days.

Greg sensed it, and when I missed another wave he shouted, "What's up with you, John? I could never beat you to a wave."

I said, "Just a little rusty, Greg. Let's go out again."

As we waited for a wave, he pressed me with, "C'mon, John. I know you better than that."

I said, "It's really hard for me to admit or even believe that the lymphoma has returned, Greg."

He replied, "I'm so sorry to hear that, John. Now what?"

"They look for a bone marrow match," I explained.

"What are the odds of that?" he asked.

I struggled as I confessed, "It's a long shot." I said this and thought about the look in Dr. Cairo's eyes. "A real long shot."

He consoled me, "John, you beat million to one odds already. You're not done. I don't feel that you're ready to leave the world yet. You have too much to accomplish and more impact to have in the world of cancer by living rather than dying and joining Erin. Yours is a story of miracles and answered prayer, not only when you made it to UCLA, but also when you were drafted in the first round of the NBA." Greg was right.

My third bout with Non-Hodgkins Lymphoma became a lesson in relationships. I realized how kind humans can be to one another, sometimes for no reason at all. I didn't merely appreciate generosity. I was dependent on it. Once again, I required a team of doctors and nurses to monitor and care for me. Beyond the people who became a daily part of my life through testing and rehabilitation, I was sustained by a network of people near and far and buoyed by phone calls and e-mails and letters and prayers.

The things I learned about deferring to a team as a twenty-one year old basketball player came to determine the success of my recovery. I had an epiphany when I came to understand I didn't just live with them, I lived for them. In the grandest and most divine connection of all, the only reason I had a chance to keep living and breathing was thanks to a gift provided by a man I still had not met.

One thing I discovered was that I had a powerful network. Once word of my diagnosis got out, I started receiving phone calls again from friends and former teammates. I was excited to hear the voice of my teammate, Kareem Abdul-Jabbar.

"I'm thinking about you, John," he said.

"I think about you too, Kareem."

He continued, "I'm always grateful for the passes you threw me in the post, and if you ever need an assist from me, I'm there for you."

I replied, "You set some nice screens for me Kareem, and this call feels like you just created an open shot for me again."

That call took me back in time. For a moment, I felt like that invincible twenty-one year old collegiate athlete. We talked about our careers, which had been very different. While we both had significant victories, we each agreed that when it gets to this point, nobody is interested in your career, the size of your house, what car you drive, or anything else you've owned or achieved.

I told him, "The only thing that matters are the people like you, Kareem, who care, show up, or say a prayer when you can't do anything to repay them. Thanks for showing up, Kareem, and being a lifelong teammate".

I was grateful that I had remained friends with this special player.

I couldn't afford to simply sit around and ponder the philosophical meaning of my plight. We needed to find a practical approach to beating this disease. The best place to get the procedure would be the MD Anderson Medical center in Houston. It was almost hard to believe that in the shadows of the arena where I played as a Houston Rocket, I would now fight for my life. Dr. Champlin, Head of Transplantation at MD Anderson and my transplant physician, signed onto the international donor registry.

We would need to find a suitable donor. My son, my sister, and other family members were tested. They didn't fit the scientific ten-part criteria for a blood cell match. Studies suggest that as much as 99.9 percent of our DNA has the same sequence. The variances between races and ethnicities can be found in that miniscule 0.1 percent of our genetic makeup. I had spent my life trying to play up the similarities between us all, and now I was being held hostage by the tiniest of differences, even within my own family.

He said that at any given time there are 6,000 people who need a bone marrow or stem cell transplant from among the millions of potential donors who are registered. We need even more donors to sign up. The odds are particularly stacked against smaller ethnic groups. For example, my friends who were black and Filipino had a child that needed a transplant and couldn't find a suitable match.

My family background is primarily Irish, with a trace of German on my paternal grandmother's side. That little trace was evidently enough to bring my genetic makeup in line with a man from Germany, who wound up matching all ten of the criteria required. This match made me realize that God was with me and was watching over every detail of my life. Of the 100 prospects who matched up well with me, Dr. Champlin determined this would be the best one.

Then the calls and the lighthearted jokes began from my UCLA teammates. I heard jokes such as, "Maybe it was Dirk Nowitzki, the German-born star of the Dallas Mavericks, and your jump shot would improve once you got his blood", "If this German guy passed the ball, would you finally do the same?", and "Would this guy's stem cells transfer some speed and jumping ability to you?"

The best response was, "Whenever you mess up at home, you could blame the mistakes on the German guy."

The plan was to do three chemotherapy treatments in Orange County then head to Houston for the transplant. The first one came before Thanksgiving. Everything about this treatment would be more difficult and more risky. The chemotherapy sessions were harsher and were made even more difficult when I developed a blood clot in my left arm. Karen turned into a nurse and gave me blood-thinning shots in my stomach twice a day. The chemo sessions, while severe, fulfilled their purpose, and I was giving thanks to be cancer-free again.

It was time for more transition. We had to load up the car and head down to Houston to set up our home base there to prepare for the transplant and recovery. We left Newport Beach on February 19 and spent three days driving to Houston, where I would receive the transplant.

In Houston, it was hard to believe that my one-time NBA body was failing me physically in the same city where I was a professional athlete.

I was mentally prepared just as I would have been for the Rockets opening tip off versus the Lakers, especially after Karen prayed for me and whispered, "I love you, John Vallely."

My transplant procedure was set for March 10th at 9:30 a.m.

First they installed a central venous catheter in my chest about ninety minutes before the procedure in order to flush my bloodstream. While it was starting, I felt a cool sensation on my chest. Even in my nervous and distracted state, I could tell something was wrong. Sure enough the line had ruptured, and blood was spilling out of it and pooling on the floor. The IV team couldn't fix the line. An alarm sounded, and it seemed like confusion as the team was shuffling around. We had been so fortunate to find a perfect donor match. What if the line ruptured again during the transplant and the precious plasma leaked out? I kept my balance. Dr. Champlin showed up, removed the old line, and installed a new one just like a pro. He assured me that these things had happened before without any problem, and they gave me a sedative to calm my anxious thoughts.

Within thirty minutes, they brought down the miracle cells for transplant.

It was one pint of plasma flown in directly from Germany. My best shot at survival was in that bag. I was starting from scratch. My blood counts registered at zero, with no red cells, no white cells, and just plasma. They hung the bag, hooked it up to an IV, and slowly began the process of replenishing my body's essential fluid. Drip by drip over the course of an hour, the bag emptied into me. As Karen observed, it was the gift of life.

The plan for the next ten days called for the cells to start multiplying and then graft to adapt to my body. There are a number of things that can go wrong in these delicate early stages and beyond.

One of these is that signs of graft versus host disease indicate that the body and its new cells are at war with each other. There can be rashes and skin sores, trouble with cataracts, respiratory distress, or the vital organs can reject the cells and shut down.

I was fortunate. I got through without a high temperature or infection. Within a day, I was up and walking around. They had color-coded cards on the hospital door to monitor my progress. Green meant fine, yellow was stable but caution, and red required immediate and special attention. I felt incredibly tired which concerned me, but my card stayed green the entire time.

As a former athlete, I had pushed myself beyond limits, but this fatigue was unimaginable. I still had toxins from the chemotherapy plus antibiotics floating through my system. Two days after the transplant, I went off the deep end. I didn't feel like I could continue. I was in a bizarre state, and I felt there was no way out. I didn't have a sense of making any progress. I felt stuck in the hospital and eternally betrayed by my body. I was completely lost, as if my soul had been wiped away.

Maybe it was simply a case of battle fatigue. The pain had gotten so bad that I had to get morphine. When the morphine mixed with the other post-transplant drugs floating through my system, it caused major vomiting. It was chaotic.

It took all I had just to get up, stand, and walk around a few steps. I craved rest, but every fifteen minutes a nurse came in to take my blood pressure and temperature. The slightest fever would be a sign of something gone wrong. I'll admit, I was whiny. I wanted for this all to be over and to get better right away.

Even the tests to measure progress could be painful, such as the double bone marrow aspiration measure test. This involved a local anesthetic to the skin, another shot, and finally a deeper shot to numb the hip bone before a corkscrew was pushed into the bone for a sample of the bone marrow in each hip. It felt like a sharp sucking or dragging sensation.

Karen tried to remind me, "John, think of how far we have come in three years of battling the disease."

I grumbled, "It's not just this transplant or this hospital stay! It's the previous transplant! All of the chemotherapy before and after! It's the mental setback of being told I have to go through it all over again."

Karen looked at me and like a great coach and general manager she shot back, "Okay, are you done being whiny, John? I'm calling Coach."

She was serious, and she dialed the hospital room phone. I knew she heard his voice because she was smiling.

"Hi, Coach."

She was good at blending an element of the serious with her sarcastic tone. "Coach, can you please talk to your player? That's right, my husband. He's breaking the set of three, Coach. Yes, whining and complaining. Nice to hear your voice too, Coach. Here's John."

She handed me the phone. "Hi, Coach. Yes, Coach, Karen is right. I've tried to do everything properly and somehow, in some way, I feel lost. I feel like I'm running a post basketball practice conditioning drill that has no end. I'm losing hope and belief that something good will come of my efforts."

He replied, "Hardship and struggle are the times when you will find faith, not when life is operating smoothly."

"Coach, I feel like I've lost my faith. After all, it isn't irrational to wonder why He is allowing all this to happen. And why does it seem that He doesn't care?"

It was time for a life lesson, and I needed this like it was 1969.

Coach continued, "In 1944 during World War II, I had orders to board the USS Franklin in the South Pacific, but my orders were canceled due to an emergency surgery. My appendix ruptured. During an

The Pyramid Principle

attack, the person who took my place was at the battle station where I would've been, and he was killed by a kamikaze pilot."

He continued, "Years later, I traveled from Atlanta to Raleigh for a summer basketball camp at Campbell University. I usually went on a Saturday, but I couldn't leave because of a conflict. I had my ticket, but I had to cancel and book the same flight for the following day. The one I was supposed to be on, the Saturday flight, crashed and everyone on board was killed, John. And flying over the crash site the next day made me consider the spiritual nature of life."

He concluded, "I thought deeply about God and His plans and wondered why He had spared me. But I know that God's hand is at work in my life and that He has plans for me. He has plans for you too, John."

I took it all in, and there was silence for a moment.

He said, "Fight the good fight, finish the race, and keep your faith, John. It will return."

"Thanks for still being my Coach," I said.

I needed to hear this from someone who had strong faith and who had a sincere belief that God has us on this earth to do certain work.

God could have taken me out of the trial, but He met me in it. In my honesty, my anger, and my doubts, He didn't need me to be perfect. He just wanted me to know Him, so I took steps to believe again.

A divine sequence of events began to unfold.

M.D. Anderson is a large medical center with twenty-five buildings, and a facility of that size requires patience. In our case, one of the seemingly endless sitting sessions at the hospital resulted in new friends, a temporary home, a local support team, and even a new miniature dachshund puppy named Doodle. That puppy followed Karen all around and would become an invaluable member of the team and our family as a support animal.

The Hillmans were an answer above and beyond Karen's endless prayers. We met Dick Hillman, his daughter Cyndi, and her husband Jim Fish, who had built a home a year earlier and included an attached apartment for such medical emergencies as ours. They gifted this apartment for us to use rent-free, which was significant as we were looking at spending five figures for housing at the Marriott.

As if all that weren't enough, Dick, Cyndi, and Jim invited thirty-five neighbors and church friends to the house and introduced us to our extended support system, who were also praying for my recovery.

My general manager Karen brought a team together and led us with team spirit. She was the rock that made this all happen. For some reason, she kept putting me back together again, along with the wonderful friends who prayed. I wondered where I would be without the prayers of my amazing wife and supportive friends.

Initially, I wondered if it could have been delirium from the medication, but God's voice was clear when I heard Him ask me, "What do you think about all those people who are praying for you?"

My first response was, "I would give anything to be as healthy as them." Then I broke the silence and said aloud, "Thank You for them."

I prayed a little louder, "Thank You, God."

I heard Him say, "I think you should pray for them in return, John."

When I prayed those prayers, I felt God's presence as surges of energy went through my body and soul. It was as if all of the prayers and wishes I had for those who were praying for me were returning back to me.

I kept praying, and I was calling them out by name saying, "God, I pray for the Fish family, for Coach Wooden, for Greg and his wife

Lynne, and for my teammates Henry, Kareem, Jerry Norman" and called them all by name. I continued, "Dr. Cairo, Dr. Champlin..." The list was going on and on, and I was excited for His hand to impact their lives as their support had impacted mine.

I was moving forward, and Dr. Champlin was positive about my progress. The engraftment continued on or ahead of schedule. Like a disciplined athlete, my days started by getting up at 5:30 a.m. Karen was always up earlier than me to get everything ready. I had breakfast with pills and headed to the cancer clinic for my blood test. Then it was more pills and off to the infusion clinic, which usually took three to five hours. If the unbearable breakfast pills didn't kill me, then lunch with more pills might.

I started walking in the morning for twenty minutes while hooked to my IV pole, took another walk when I got home, and then took a third walk in the evening. I started physical therapy and was grateful that the fatigue was not as bad as it had been during my first stem cell transplant two years earlier. At the same time, it had been over three months since I felt healthy. I knew the preparation is where my success would be found, and I also knew that one of Coach's favorite sayings was, "The journey is better than the end." It was in this journey that I returned to competitive greatness by learning to love a difficult challenge.

As I thought back to Erin's plea, "Pray for me, Daddy," I realized that self-sufficiency was a myth created by temporary success. Erin taught me that God's power is made perfect in weakness, so I continued to pray with industriousness for my recovery. I also continued to pray for those who I knew by name and offered so much support through all of my life's challenges. I prayed that they could continue to live lives that were blessed in ways they didn't even realize because I knew time spent in good health was the most important thing in life. I prayed for the people I knew only by face, such as the smiling, kind hearted women who came in and took blood samples from me and hundreds of patients a day.

I would find that my body, which had carried me from Orange Coast College to the heights of collegiate basketball and from the depths of cancer to life again, could handle the impact of one more grueling comeback.

The days now started with a simple prayer such as, "God, walk with me step-by-step, move me forward in my recovery, give me strength to fight and tolerate all the medication, and help me to be patient through the fatigue. Help me trust You and have faith in Your plan for my life. Take away the fear of my future, and please help Karen. Give her Your strength for all she has to do today. And say hi to Erin, and tell her that her eternal smiling face always encourages me. Thank you, Lord, for the new day."

I finally had a sense that tomorrow would be better than today. I couldn't wait to find out what tomorrow had in store. It was a euphoric feeling like I was living life on the highest level.

Prayer became a special part of my days and gave me energy to go through this battle. It was such a lift to be able to return my prayers for all of those who were lifting me in their prayers. I received a very special blessing. It came in the form of peace from my innermost being, as all the unimportant things in my life got stripped away. Eventually, my body began to improve as well. With hope and optimism, I couldn't wait for the next day to see if this energy added to my healing experience.

Eric called me and asked how I was feeling. I said, "I feel good to be alive, Eric, but we're not even a genetic match anymore. My blood now has more in common with a fifty-five-year-old German, who doesn't speak a word of English."

Like my teammates, Eric had jokes and said, "I wish I could have gotten that guy's vertical for the volleyball court." Then, with the sound of some tears in his voice, he continued, "But I'm glad I was born to you. You have been an amazing dad, and I'm so grateful we have had this life together. And we have more years ahead."

I said, "I love you, Eric. I'm so proud to be your dad."

It made it all worthwhile to hear my son's voice that day. It was one more reason to keep fighting.

The longer I was in there, the more I was driven to get out. I was exhausted, but Karen continued to remind me, "John, Coach once told me to tell you to 'Move, move, move!' And this is my reminder to get out there and move!"

I had to find a method to measure my victories, and as I walked in the hallways of the hospital, I gauged the distance traveled by hospital landmarks. I would add a few room numbers to the distance I would travel each day.

It was a tough hit for a guy who had competed among the world's greatest athletes in the NBA to be winded by a short walk. As I thought back to my conditioning work for UCLA in preparation for the start of training camp, I drew strength from what Coach had taught me. He would pace up and down the sidelines at practice shouting, "Nothing will work unless you do, John!"

Our friends Greg and Lynne George came to visit us in Houston. Far from the days when we were preparing for USC and UCLA and training step-by-step, my rehabilitation now consisted of a painful and wobbly hobble down the hallway where Greg saw me hunched over with hands on my knees and breathing heavily. He was waving a USC T-shirt in his hands, and I couldn't think of a worse way to begin this conversation than to battle over the pre-eminence of UCLA.

I shouted, "Did Henry Bibby put you up to this?"

It was never small talk with Greg, and I wouldn't want it anyway. I waited for his banter about UCLA, armed with "University of Spoiled Children" as my comeback.

It was worse as he threw that toxic colored T-shirt in my direction and said, "No. But you won't believe what my school is doing for your pediatric cancer research."

I really didn't have any energy for a comeback, so he kept talking with a glimmer in his eyes about a sponsored event that had just taken place at USC called "Dribble for the Cure," which is now called "Dribble for Victory over Cancer." It was an excitement from him that I had not seen since his signing for USC football.

He explained, "It began at Marquette University in the 70's by basketball coach Al McGuire, but USC brought it back. At the event, local athletes of all ages seek sponsorship from individuals and businesses and spend the day dribbling on USC's campus to raise money for pediatric cancer research. And let me tell you, John, it was awesome!"

Now he had my attention. He continued his impassioned explanation.

"And not only did the men's and women's basketball teams participate and sign autographs while the band and the cheerleaders performed, but also my football team participated, which gave this day even greater significance." I was getting a vision.

He kept going, "And the volleyball team, swimming, track and field, baseball and softball teams as well. It was like the competitive drive of the USC sports program had rallied to battle cancer, and I couldn't wait to come to tell you about it! and tell you to keep battling, John, and 'fight on'!"

Normally, I would break into a "UCLA 4 clap," but on this day I responded, "Fight on, Greg!" With zero sarcasm intended this time, I threw up the "V" hand sign for USC Victory.

I followed that with a touch of sarcasm and said, "But what did you do at the event, Greg? I know you can't dribble." We both laughed. It was good to laugh and dream that day.

My purpose was renewed. I put on that "USC Dribble for Victory" shirt, and Greg walked with me that day as I picked up my step. Eventually, like a twenty-one year old UCLA athlete again, I turned that rehab into a full-blown workout in MD Anderson's Physical Therapy Center. What a beautiful USC T-shirt that was!

I spent the next several days imagining what "Dribble for Victory Over Cancer" could become at UCLA and around the country, and I surprisingly felt re-energized.

I wouldn't waste the pain of Erin's death. I wouldn't squander the agony of Non-Hodgkin's Lymphoma and a stem cell transplant. I was going to amplify the meaning of the sport that led me to UCLA, with this event's namesake. I recalled all those hours on the court, in the sand, in the Alley, and the unfulfilled career ending in Belgium. At that moment, I was aware that "God causes all things to work for good, to those who love Him, to those called according to His purpose."

It got me through all of the hard work yet to come and the increasingly difficult rehab sessions that expanded to include stationary bike riding and weight training. As tired as I felt, all it took was a look around the physical therapy room to realize how good I had it and how far I had come. Some patients could not get out of their wheelchair, some could not lift their arms, and others could not even see. I was grateful to have the function of my legs and arms.

Thirteen days after the transplant, with the new cells "engrafted" into my system, I was on the road to recovery. A few days later, when my blood counts reached a satisfactory level, I was released from the hospital. We had to remain in Houston until we hit the 100-day mark just to make sure there were no complications.

There was a great pay-off: the results were good and the blood counts were improving. The donor cells had taken over my immune system. In a sense, the old John Vallely was no more.

I didn't even know the donor man's name. Donors and recipients are initially kept anonymous for security reasons. In the past, there have been situations when the recipient needed more stem cells, and the donor withheld them while demanding more money like a sort of biological ransom.

I still wrote a letter to my anonymous angel to be passed along to him.

"My wife and I really love each other, and to have more time together means so much to us," I wrote. "You are responsible for giving us the opportunity to carry on. We regard you as an angel, and we thank God for you and your willingness to share of yourself. May all good things come to you and your family. So far, so good with my transplant. Thank you again."

After three months, our time in Houston was finishing up. We packed up the car and headed home with a new perspective on life and a new four-legged member of the family named Doodle, the Fish's miniature dachshund who fell in love with Karen.

I thought of my brief time on the Houston Rockets, and as we traveled west on Interstate 10, I thought of our second apartment and turned left onto Central Park West.

We passed the location where we once lived, and I asked Karen, "If you could do it over, would you do anything differently?"

She responded, "Nothing. Coach was right, the journey is better than the end."

After a brief silence she said, "There is one thing I would change. It would be my made up fortune cookie to say, 'Every good and perfect gift comes from above.'" With that, she grabbed my hand.

I've had people congratulate me for "kicking cancer's butt," yet no one kicks cancer's butt. It extracts too much from you. You don't emerge feeling victorious, but you do feel grateful and know that it wasn't you alone that did it. It was the team that did it and all of the people who gave me another chance at life, including the medical staff, Karen, and Coach Wooden who taught me to compete. I was elated to finally be moving forward with my life.

I still wondered why I had been allowed to survive this and not my daughter. I didn't feel regret because I had no control over it, and God's ways are a mystery and not always understood. I am confident of this: that I will see the goodness of the Lord in this present life, so I take heart and wait patiently for Him.

Chapter 18

HALL OF FAME INDUCTION

"If you were fortunate enough to have played for Coach and stayed in touch with him, you have a mentor and friend for life."

~ John Vallely

In 2006, I was inducted into the UCLA Hall of Fame. I was overwhelmed to see Coach Wooden now seated in the front row as I spoke and gave testimony to everything he taught me. His teachings had led me to the NBA and to competitive greatness; his principles led me to faith and wisdom that helped me win a battle against a bank and success in the second half of my life. They played my short highlight video, and it gave me a moment to reflect on this journey and the first team meeting with Coach Wooden thirty-five years ago. The highlight video included the Drake clip and the kick out from Kareem. It seemed like it had just happened yesterday.

I wondered if the player who tossed the paper airplane at me had come to understand "success." I wondered if my teammates still tied their shoes properly.

"Thank you all very much. I consider it a great honor to be inducted into the UCLA Hall of Fame," I said. "In the journey of life, an athletic career is one chapter of a much larger book. But it has been my experiences in sports that have influenced every aspect of my life. Nothing has a higher place of significance than the approach to life that I learned from the greatest teacher of the twentieth century, Coach John Wooden."

I continued, "If you were fortunate enough to have played for Coach and stayed in touch with him, you have a mentor and friend for life. Most important for me has been his Pyramid of Success. Success is not the attainment of wealth, power, or political position as the world defines it. It's the peace of mind that comes from knowing you did your best, to become the best you are capable of becoming, in sports, marriage, business, parenting, and life."

My words became more personal as I shared, "When we lost our daughter Erin to cancer at age twelve, the loss was huge and still hurts today. But in a way, we felt that we were successful because we played the game of life at the highest level. Our entire family gave everything we could give."

"Some of you may not know this," I said, "but I have been fighting my own battle with cancer. And after a failed transplant using my own stem cells, I have received stem cells from a fifty-five year old German guy, and I am happy to report his stem cells are working! During this battle, I lost one of the most important parts of the Pyramid. I told Coach, 'I have no hope. I have lost my faith.' Within a second, this wise man responded, 'Be patient, John. Your faith will return.' And it did. Is that not council for a lifetime?"

I said, "For most of my life, I have been fortunate enough to surround myself with wonderfully talented people with character. One of those is my wife and my best friend Karen, who has given me such incredible support and inspiration. Another one is our amazing son Eric, who is a constant source of strength. I have also leaned heavily on my friends and family, many of whom are here tonight. I've drawn strength from the relationships I have with my UCLA family, Coach John Wooden, Coach Jerry Norman, who recruited me, my teammates, and many other players."

I concluded, "You have all meant everything to me while I have been in this fight for my life. The prayers, emails, letters, phone calls, and words of encouragement from all of you are the reason I'm able to be part of this induction ceremony. It makes me very happy to be here tonight. I love you all. Thank you for such a special honor."

Bill Walton stood up and led a standing ovation, and it was a sharp contrast to the polite clap they gave me after the brief highlight video.

I sensed that my story had more meaning than my career, where I hit a few jump shots and made a few passes. I won't tell you that the UCLA moments weren't some of the highlights of my life or that NBA draft day wasn't a rush for this surf rat. Yet, success had taken on new meaning and become bigger than the trophies I had received and greater than the battles I had won.

Bill approached me and said, "You have to tell your story, John!" I was grateful that this legend acknowledged me that day. He passed away on May 27th after his own long fight with cancer. He was a good friend and supporter of Pediatric Cancer Research. I was sorry that the world's efforts were not enough to affect his survival rate.

Chapter 19
LOVE

"The most important thing in the world is family and love."

~ Coach John Wooden

On June 4th, 2010, I was back on the campus thinking about Coach Wooden in the front row as I entered the Hall. This time I would be watching him pass from this life to enter eternal life, in his last moments at UCLA Medical.

At UCLA Medical, the court wins don't matter. The only UCLA blue in the room is the medical scrubs of the hospital staff, and the teams in this arena fight every day for greater causes than the games at the basketball arena down the street.

Outside Coach's hospital room, I had only a moment to decide what to say to someone who had influenced every aspect of my life, from marriage, family, and career to surviving life and death. I came back to the one thing that he held up above everything: love. We entered his room. Despite his frail condition, I could only remember the strength and speed of the coach who ran down from the top row of the bleachers to command me to pass the ball to the sideline cutter.

I composed myself and said, "Coach, it's Team Vallely. I just want to thank you for everything you did for me and mostly for commanding me to marry this amazing woman." Barely conscious, Coach still managed a smile. "We love you, Coach," I said.

His eyes did not open, and he struggled to whisper back, "I love you."

We sat and held his hand for a while, and the next day he was gone. Karen and I held each other and sobbed. First we cried tears of sadness and then tears of joy, as Karen reminded me, "We will see him again."

We are conditioned as athletes to work, compete, hustle, rise, and overcome. We know how to bounce back from a loss versus USC, and we know how to return to the arena from major sports surgeries. We have learned how to recover when we're down by six points with two minutes left. We know how to rely on coaches and teammates who can give the answers or provide solutions when we are weak.

Coach was insightful to put "faith through prayer" at the top of his Pyramid.

Despite his ten championships, he knew there were times when a competitor's foundation was strong. He knew that you could stand at the edge of greatness and yet feel desperate. He understood that sometimes we lack the right answers, the strong team, or the will to fight.

We can't always work harder or smarter, and our determined efforts are not always enough for the challenge. Yet, in these times it is possible to find greatness by patiently praying with faith for a power that you don't possess. It is in that very weakness when you realize that God's greatness is more than you can ask or imagine, and it is He alone who can bring you through.

Chapter 20
THE GIFT
OF LIFE

"I don't think the way you think. The way you work isn't the way I work. For as the sky soars high above the earth, so the way I work surpasses the way you work, and the way I think is beyond the way you think."
~ Isaiah 55:8-9 (MSG)[10]

With the passing of Coach Wooden, I reflected on the frailty of my own existence but was also reminded that I still had more to do with this life. I knew Coach had conditioned me for a second half, and I wanted to pass on his teachings in his memory.

We were eventually given the identity of my stem cell donor's name and his contact information from the Registry. His name was Richard Hoffmeister. Richard lived in Germany, and I knew that I had to meet the man who gave me the gift of my life. I wanted to thank him in person and let him see the life that he had allowed me to continue.

We were thrilled to find out that Richard's daughter Katrin was working in Connecticut, and Richard was planning a visit. We arranged to meet him there, with his daughter serving as the translator. It was a beautiful autumn day, and the two lane highway led us through an explosion of crimson, orange, gold, and purple leaves that paved our trail to the red brick house.

No words needed to be spoken between Karen and me, but I was aware that this forty-year love affair could not be derailed by death, cancer, or loss.

I would never have experienced the gift of life that Hofmeister gave me without the love of this beautiful woman and force of nature sitting next to me. She refused to let me falter or feel sorry for myself and compelled me to "move." The team spirit she brought to my basketball career and to my life made me unstoppable and carried me through life and death.

When we arrived at the home, Richard opened the door. I was surprised to be looking up at someone six feet four inches. He was even taller than me.

I immediately wrapped him up in a big hug and exclaimed, "Richard, you have saved my life. I would not be here these last three years if you had not given your precious gift."

I'm sure it caught him off guard, but then Katrin translated my words. He lit up with a huge smile, and we all hugged. The connection was immediate and intense just as I hoped it would be.

We proceeded to the living room and met the rest of the family members. Karen brought out pictures that included everything from my days in the Houston hospital receiving Richard's stem cells to our vacation relaxing in Hawaii just a few weeks earlier.

Katrin said, "My father learned of the donor program when a young girl in a village near his home in Germany was diagnosed with cancer, and a call for blood, stem cells, and bone marrow went out to the surrounding towns." I immediately thought of that young girl and imagined that she was much like Erin. I would pray for her and her family.

Katrin continued, "Moved by the plea, my father responded and went to have his blood drawn, tested, and entered into the International Registry. When he showed up as a match for someone, his blood was drawn and run through a blood separator, which harvested five million stem cells."

"The next day they were delivered to my bedside in Houston, and the life-saving process began. What a miracle you are," I whispered through my sobbing.

We spent four hours together that night learning about each other and taking pictures. I could feel the powerful bond and our dependence on each other. In my case, it had never been so abundantly clear.

Richard's wife Angelica cooked an amazing traditional German meal, and Richard pulled out a bottle of Cabernet Sauvignon wine.

Katrin said, "I hope you like red wine. My father is a fourth generation red wine maker, and this wine is from his vineyard."

"My favorite!" I answered.

We raised our glasses in a "toast to life," and I was suddenly hit with the overwhelming significance of Erin's last words before her passing, which were, "What kind of wine do you like, Dad?"

Some may call it luck or coincidence, but when I consider my marathon journey, it all comes back to that sliver of "faith through prayer" from Coach Wooden's Pyramid of Success. It is clear that not only did God heal me and provide for me, but He really was "in that very room" with Erin. On this side of heaven, I'll never understand why our daughter did not receive the same gift of earthly healing that I did. It felt surreal to meet the man whose stem cells saved my life and to hear that his call to the donation came from a needful young female cancer patient like Erin had been. It left me with only one response to the God Who had connected us, which was to be grateful for such a miracle.

I kept that red wine bottle to remind me that God is great, and His ways are limitless.

Everyday I still have to check my attitude, and when I don't, Karen reminds me of Coach Wooden's thoughts on attitude.

"Things turn out best for those who make the best of the way things turn out."

It helps when I realize that I can only control my effort and my attitude. Beyond that, I give my path to the same sovereign God Who led me to a bone marrow donor in Germany.

I can't always figure things out in order to gain a sense of mastery over my life. Human understanding cannot bring me peace. Yet, I've learned much from the book of Proverbs in the Bible. I trust God from the bottom of my heart and resist trying to figure everything out on my own. I listen to God's voice in everything I do and look for Him everywhere I go because He is the one Who will keep me on track.

Coach taught me to follow wholeheartedly wherever he led, with a quickening of my pace. In my twenty one year old mind, the shot or the dribble drive made sense because I didn't know what better options were ahead. Coach saw the game's development and the pass or the hard cut to the basket that led to better opportunities offensively. His thoughts were much more forward-thinking on outcomes than mine.

Some of God's blessings are beyond our sight but are still near and very real. We are not to close our eyes to the reality of the pain that is around us. Sometimes He leads us up a high mountain in Belgium or in Seattle on an exhausting road that seems destined for disaster. The more faith I give to these high climbs, the more brilliant my view, and the more I sense a departure from the world with its problems. Like Coach Wooden watching practice from the top row of the arena, I see life differently from God's perspective.

Chapter 21

"DRIBBLE FOR VICTORY OVER CANCER"

"You can't live a perfect day without doing something for someone who will never be able to repay you."

~ John Vallely

I'm certain that God envisioned that day when I made my first shot in my Balboa Island alleyway. I know he saw my first swish at Pauley Pavilion.

I am convinced that He saw the day we would arrive at "Dribble For Victory Over Cancer" to set up an eight foot flag that displayed Erin's picture as the event's honorary captain. I know He has kept track of my sadness and recorded each tear in His ledger and each ache in His book. He knew that Erin's life and legacy would impact many.

As athletes with basketballs started to arrive from various schools around Los Angeles, I was moved by the outpouring of support and touched by the familiar sound of the dribbling balls. UCLA athletes signed autographs, local kids met their favorite players, and the band played the UCLA fight song. As participants registered at the entry, they were given safety pins for a page for a personal show of support that read: "I dribble for ___". One by one, the athletes and coaches who came to raise money for the cure filled in the name of a loved one, family member, or friend and pinned the page on the back of their shirt. Some of the people behind these printed names were currently battling cancer, some had won their battle, and others had passed away. Eric's daughter Vivi, who strongly resembled Erin, asked me to help her pin one on her back. I wept as I pinned it on her strong shoulders and saw the words, "I dribble for Erin."

Nell Everett from ESPN served as the event emcee and introduced the various UCLA teams, coaches, and players, who all rallied on their day off to support this event. It was not just men's and women's basketball. It was also football, volleyball, baseball, softball, track, swimming, and cheerleading. The response was overwhelming.

Neil introduced Kenny Thomas, a healthy fifteen year old athlete, whose life and message represented the spirit of the event. Kenny stepped towards the crowd and said, "I want to thank you all for being here today because I am a cancer survivor." The crowd gave him a thunderous ovation. He continued, "At age ten, I was diagnosed with a life threatening cancer. But this year as a high school freshman, I made the school basketball team for the first time. This never would have happened without you and the support of the Pediatric Cancer Research Foundation." The participants cheered wildly again with a greater understanding of this event's reach and meaning.

The participants were dismissed to start their dribbling.

The dribbling wove through the campus, and that beautiful chorus of bouncing basketballs brought me back to my time at UCLA, especially as I spoke with a number of former players. Among them was Jerry Norman, whose recruitment led me here. As Coach Wooden had once directed me to do from his post up in the UCLA stands, I kept my eyes upwards and looked ahead. What I saw ahead of me in life was wide open.

The big dribbling event would end up on the court at Pauley Pavilion, which took me past Coach Wooden's recently constructed life-size statue. As I walked by his image, I could envision the Pyramid of Success on his office wall. I could feel my shoelaces tightening, and I could see Erin running to say hello to Coach at games. I could hear his powerful voice and feel his strong hand in my heart as he commanded me, "You marry that girl." Now I walked on campus forty-five years later, with Karen still by my side, Coach Wooden's hand still on my life, and Erin's presence among us in a powerful way.

Inside Pauley Pavilion, the gameday energy filled the arena, as the Vice President of Business Development for the PCRF, Jeri Wilson stepped up to the podium. Jeri's mission was to raise awareness and funding for pediatric cancer research, as she cultivated donors throughout the country, with her strong business mind, But it was Jeri's team spirit, and servant heart that made her a force of nature in this battleground for children's lives, and an integral part in counseling families through their grief related to this horrible disease, including Karen and I.

It was Jeri's privilege to award the top individual fundraisers, schools who raised money for the cure as a team, and individuals who joined up as a team for this cause.

I had to collect myself as the next award to be given was the "Erin Vallely Courage Award." Jeri was the right person to pass me the award, as she understood not only the magnitude of Erin's loss, but also the immensity of her influence. As I held the award, I ran my fingers over Erin's name, forever ingrained on this award and on my heart. UCLA women's basketball coach, Cori Close who had previously won this award was called up to present. And, as I handed that award to Cori, I could feel Erin's life surge through my hand.

Cori was a close friend and a disciple of Coach Wooden. She briefly talked about Coach's influence on her faith and her powerful coaching career, which has led her to the top ten of the NCAA rankings. Cori said, "I'm very proud of my UCLA players and all of you who are here today to help defeat this opponent. I learned many powerful lessons from Coach Wooden and John Vallely, who taught me that 'the only things that will stay with you from athletics are who you become and who you impact.' Because of that, I'm happy to present the 'Erin Vallely Courage Award' to Doctor Ted Moore, the Chief of Pediatric Hematology/Oncology and the Director of Pediatric Blood and Marrow Transplant Program at UCLA."

As he received the award, Dr. Moore spoke, "Thank you, Cori. Thanks, John. Thanks to all of you who are fighting this enemy. When we first started, children with cancer had very little hope for survival. Today, overall survival exceeds eighty-five percent and the mortality rate has declined by more than fifty percent. We look forward to the future with many stories like this one standing here with me today. This is Tae Butler, a cancer survivor, who I met when she was a nine year old cancer patient and was receiving treatment at UCLA Mattel's Children Hospital. Now cancer free, Tae is currently a fourth year UCLA Medical student and a role model of courage and strength."

The crowd roared, and he continued, "Tae is now assisting me as a research assistant and carrying on the research that began because of Erin, John, and Karen Vallely's commitment to pediatric research funding. The funds that you have all helped to raise today will make a huge impact."

The crowd burst into applause again, and I could only compare that ovation to the feeling I had when I ran through the tunnel and onto this court against Purdue in my first game. Yet, this cheering sounded different. It was a pure and holy sound and the kind of praise that you will never feel when they applaud you for making a basket. This was an acclaim reserved for survivors, doctors, researchers, and fundraiser dribblers. That moment fueled me with a greater commitment to find the next great college basketball arenas that would host "Dribble For Victory Over Cancer."

It was overwhelming to think that the Pediatric Cancer Research Foundation's efforts played a part in the survival of this future M.D. and that Tae would spend her lifetime fighting to keep the next generation of afflicted children alive.

It was surreal when I would later find out that Tae was the daughter of UCLA basketball great Mitchell Butler. As I had once cheered for Mitchell on the court, I would now be cheering for his daughter to save lives like my daughter did through her fundraising plea at age twelve. I'm certain that the cancer-free life of Tae, another UCLA basketball player's daughter and Erin's "UCLA sister," would have given my sweet daughter great joy.

It was my turn to address the participants and the current teams. I was grateful that Coach Wooden gave me something more significant than a drive for Championships and perishable awards and had no doubt that I was here to give this crowd of athletes the wisdom that Coach Wooden would have given our team before a practice session. It was wisdom that was timeless and reciprocal, with teachings that I had passed to Erin, who lived them out and then passed them back to me.

The spotlight at the center of the "Nell and John Wooden Court" was now on me. The flood of emotions ranged from sadness to game time excitement. In this moment, I was balanced as I stepped onto the very spot on this court where Coach had once pushed me in my stance at practice.

I began, "It has been a long time since I played here for the legendary Coach Wooden and won two National Championships. Coach was a man of great wisdom, and it is his wisdom, not only his sports record, that has had a timeless influence on countless lives. He was a great teacher and taught me many things that have stayed with me on my journey such as, 'Happiness begins when selfishness ends.' One of his notable sayings to our UCLA team was, 'You can't live a perfect day without doing something for someone who will never be able to repay you.'"

I continued, "My daughter Erin fought valiantly against cancer and lost her battle at age twelve, but she believed in a cure. That little fighter battled hard for a cure. She dreamed and pleaded for the names who are pinned to your shirts. These are names of the people you love. If the Coach, who won those ten Championship banners hanging above you, was here today, he would say, 'I wish I would have put love at the top of the Pyramid of Success because love and family are the most important things in the world.'"

I finished by saying, "I thank you for contributing selflessly to cancer patients here at UCLA Mattel Children's Hospital and to patients around the world who you will never meet or know. Those young, fragile patients will have a greater chance to live because of the increased research funding that you have raised today."

The crowd erupted into cheers, and I knew my life on this court had come full circle. These cheers were for the afflicted children who could only repay us by continuing to hope, live, and experience the joy of arriving at their own personal success and peace of mind.

"Dribble for Victory Over Cancer" was truly the fulfillment of Coach Wooden's instruction to live a perfect day and Erin's plea at the Pediatric Cancer Research Gala.

Chapter 22
FAITH

"Joy is possible because death is not the end but the beginning."

~ John Vallely

For five decades, I had followed Coach Wooden and his principals, offense, work ethic, and advice on marriage, business, and faith. When you choose the hard work of real faith, the results come. It is this faith that empowers you to commit to a lifetime of marriage where you will find that love is the greatest thing. It is this faith that strengthens you to place your life savings on the line in a lawsuit so that truth might prevail. It is this faith that proves that God is powerful enough to find a bone marrow match in the red wine fields of Germany. It is this faith that presents a promise of hope that one day the pediatric cancer suffering will be eradicated. It is this faith that reassures us that earthly death has been defeated and that God has lovingly paved the way to a victorious life in heaven.

I still struggle and question. I'm still learning and growing. Yet, because of that sliver of faith at the top of the Pyramid, I'm still working through those character blocks as I rise towards success. I still need to choose joy on a daily basis, and I now know more than ever that joy is possible because death is not the end but the beginning.

One day, I'll reunite in a perfect place with a perfect love. I will see my daughter, Coach Wooden, and come face to face with the God Who answered Erin's hospital prayer and provided me with a bone marrow donor and second half in life. I have experienced the greatest wins and the greatest losses you could ever imagine. I've had people ask me over the years, "Does heaven ease the pain of Erin's death?" The answer is always, "No! The earthly pain of loss is as great as ever, but I think of that kid in the dream and have been comforted because I can fully imagine it."

I know in my head and from my experience that heaven is real. Someday I'll run towards Erin, and it won't be a dream anymore. I envision that God is there, and I am in the presence of many angels. It's brilliant and the sights and sounds eclipse the beauty of cheering and the beauty of a sailboat at sunset. I hear the song "Amazing Grace," and Erin is painting a rainbow in the sky. She sees me, runs toward me, jumps in my arms, and says, "Look at the rainbow we painted for Mom and Eric over the Pavilion today."

I'm home.

In 1993 in an ESPN event known as the ESPY Awards, coaching legend Jim Valvano took the platform with stage four cancer and two months to live. On that stage, he raised the banner powerfully for cancer research. In an emotional speech, he announced the beginning of the "V Foundation for Cancer Research," with its motto "Don't give up. Don't ever give up." Jimmy V echoed the words that Erin once spoke, "We need money for research. It may not save my life, but it may save my children's lives. It may save someone you love."

In spite of its devastating consequences, he reminded the audience to hope and think beyond the temporal when he declared to the world, "Cancer can take away all my physical abilities, but cancer cannot touch my mind It cannot touch my heart and cannot touch my soul. And those three things are going to carry on forever."

This year we partnered with the Jimmy "V" Foundation for Cancer Research, and "Dribble for Victory over Cancer" has expanded from UCLA and St. John's to Duke, UNC, and Davidson. In these iconic arenas, where we once fought for a trophy, we now fight for cancer's cure. The sound of a dribbling ball in that Balboa Island alley from my childhood now has a more profound and greater meaning. It is the sound of a child with a name pinned to the back of their shirt, dribbling on a campus somewhere to raise money and save one more life.

Erin's legacy, heart, and soul will carry on forever.

"I Dribble For Erin."

"Erin's stuffed animals Bub and Smokey who accompanied her through chemo"

"John and Karen Vallely portrait"

The Pyramid Principle

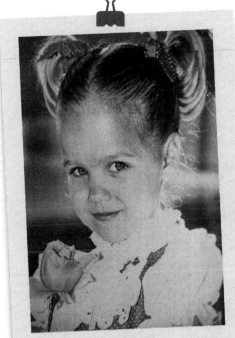

"Erin age 3"

"Eric and Erin beach day"

"Eric and daughter Vivi"

Based on the Life of John Vallely

John and Karen Vallely – 54 years of sunsets.

"Karen and John walk hand and hand 2024"

John Vallely with PCRF. org's a V.P. of Development, Jeri Wilson, and UCLA Women's Basketball coach, Cori Close at "Dribble For Victory Over Cancer."

The Pyramid Principle

John Vallely with UCLA Women's Basketball coach, Cori Close, and PCRF.org V.P. of Development, Jeri Wilson, at "Dribble For Victory Over Cancer."

PCRF.org's Jeri Wilson, John, Karen, Doodle, and Dr. Ted Moore, Chief of Pediatric Hematology/Oncology and Director of the Pediatric Blood and Marrow Transplant Program at UCLA, at "Dribble For Victory Over Cancer."

LO[

THE PYRAMID OF SUCCESS

John R. Wooden
Head Basketball Coach
UCLA

For— John & Karen Vallely two extra special people in our basketball "family" with love and best wishes to you and yours always in all ways.

John & Nell Wooden

FAITH
Through prayer

COMPETITIV[

"When the go[
the tough gets
Be at your [
your best is n[
Real love of [

FIGHT
(effort and hustle)

POISE

Just being yourself.
Being at ease in any
situation.
Never fighting yourself.

RESOURCEFULNESS
(proper judgment)

CONDITION

Mental - Moral - Physical
Rest, exercise, and diet
must be considered. Mod-
eration must be practiced.
Dissipation must be
eliminated.

SK[

A knowledg[
ability to prop[
the fundamen[
Be prepared [
detail.

ADAPTABILITY
(to any situation)

SELF-CONTROL

Emotions under control.
Delicate adjustment bet-
ween mind and body.
Keep judgment and
common sense.

ALERTNESS

Be observing constantly.
Be quick to spot a
weakness and correct it
or use it as the case may
warrant.

AMBITION
(properly focused)

INDUSTRIOUSNESS

There is no substitute for
work. Worthwhile things
come from hard work and
careful planning.

FRIENDSHIP

Comes from mutual
esteem, respect, and
devotion.
A sincere liking for
all.

LOY[

To your[
all those d[
upon you.[
self-respe[

The Pyramid Principle

VE

PATIENCE
Good things take time

INTEGRITY
(speaks for itself)

Success is peace of mind which is a direct result of self-satisfaction in knowing you did your best to become the best that you are capable of becoming.

/E GREATNESS

ing gets tough,
s going."
best when
eeded.
f a hard battle.

RELIABILITY
(others depend upon you)

CONFIDENCE

Respect without fear.
Confident, not cocky.
May come from faith in
yourself in knowing
that you are prepared.

ILL

e of and the
perly execute
itals.
. Cover every

TEAM SPIRIT

An eagerness to sacrifice
personal interests or glory
for the welfare of all.
The team comes first.

HONESTY
(in all ways)

INITIATIVE

Cultivate the ability to
make decisions and think
alone.
Desire to excel.

INTENTNESS

Ability to resist temp-
tation and stay with your
course.
Concentrate on your
objective and be determined
to reach your goal.

SINCERITY
(makes friends)

ALTY

self and to
ependent
Keep your
ct.

COOPERATION

With all levels of your
co-workers. help others
and see the other side.

ENTHUSIASM

Your heart must be in
your work.
Stimulate others.

Based on the Life of John Vallely

COLLEGE BASKETBALL'S GREATEST COACH

John Wooden, widely regarded as one of the greatest coaches in sports history, guided the UCLA Bruins to an unprecedented ten NCAA championships in twelve years, including seven consecutive titles from 1967 to 1973. His legacy goes beyond basketball; he mentored legends such as Kareem Abdul-Jabbar and Bill Walton, instilling in them the values of excellence and integrity. Wooden, who was inducted into the Naismith Memorial Basketball Hall of Fame as both a player and a coach, created the **Pyramid of Success** as a timeless framework for achieving greatness in all aspects of life, reflecting his deep commitment to personal development and character-building. As he famously stated, "Success is peace of mind that is the direct result of self-satisfaction in knowing you did your best to become the best that you are capable of becoming."

REFERENCES

[1] Moriarty, George. The Road Ahead or The Road Behind. 1919.

[2] "Ain't No Mountain High Enough." Written by Nickolas Ashford and Valerie Simpson, performed by Marvin Gaye and Tammi Terrell. © 1967 Motown Records.

[3] King, Martin Luther Jr. "I Have a Dream." Speech delivered at the March on Washington for Jobs and Freedom, Washington, D.C., August 28, 1963.

[4] Hot Fun in the Summertime" is a 1969 song recorded by Sly and the Family Stone.

[5] "Hail to the Hills of Westwood." UCLA Alma Mater, lyrics by Jeane Emerson, music by Don Wilson.

[6] "My Favorite Things" from The Sound of Music soundtrack. Lyrics by Oscar Hammerstein II, music by Richard Rodgers. © 1959 Rodgers & Hammerstein.

[7] "I Want a Hippopotamus for Christmas." Written by John Rox, performed by Gayla Peevey. © 1953 Columbia Records.

[8] Lyrics from In This Very Room by Ron and Carol Harris. © Copyright 1979 Ron Harris Music.

[9] Lyrics from "Amazing Grace" copyright 1779 by John Newton.

[10] Isaiah 55:8-9 from The Message, copyright © 1993, 2002, 2018 by Eugene H. Peterson. Used by permission of NavPress. All rights reserved. Represented by Tyndale House Publishers.

PAUL'S ACKNOWLEDGEMENTS

Thank you to John, Karen, and Eric Vallely for letting me be a part of your incredible life journey and help tell your powerful story. Thank you for living your life with competitive greatness and as an example and a testimony to your "faith through prayer." The "patience" that holds the Pyramid together held this project together as you live out Coach Wooden's Pyramid Principles in every aspect. Your story makes me believe in miracles, teamwork, prayer, and love.

Thank you to my Mom for your relentless prayers and endless support of my lifetime of crazy dreams, including Wake Forest Football, which led to this writer's dream through "Brian's Song." To my brother Steve, basketball coaching legend and Hall of Famer "Coach Wise," who believed in and supported the journey, your life and career influence makes me believe in this story and its message.

To writing partner Grace Westlin, thank you for believing in this project at the counter of Vernetti. Thank you for showing up to write with an untested novelist and preparing for a "red letter game" that was not scheduled yet. Thanks for bringing inspiration, creative magic, a voice, a muse, and a much needed editor's skillset to a desk so I could create while driving that thirteen miles of magic on Sunset Blvd. You represent Coach Wooden's "team spirit" at the highest level.

Thank you to Art Leeds, who "played" for Coach Wooden and set legal screens for years to get me open to "heave up" shots, until we made this shot. You are a pure swish shooter with a rhythmic dribble. Thanks to Bill Ewing, a studio legend, who looked ahead to the sideline cutter and gave me the perfect assist while teaching me story, structure, and the importance of "writing is rewriting is rewriting" towards building a "masterpiece." Thank you for remaining undying in your support and prayer while dealing with my rough drafts as we moved this story towards the screen. Thanks to Izzy Centeno, who created endless master-

ACKNOWLEDGEMENTS

piece versions of publisher and film pitch decks while disregarding my plea, "Just ten pages, Izzy." Thanks to Keith Osburn for your relentless search for film partners, which led to this publishing partner. Thanks to Alfred Hopton for your belief without evidence. You are a team of All-American producing partners.

Thank you to publisher CEO Kevin White for believing in this story. You came into the game and added quick points and energy to the team. Thank you for your faithful response to God's calling in Psalm 96:3, "Publish God's glorious deeds, tell everyone about the amazing things He does." You are the best new publisher in the game.

To agent Greg Ray, thanks for believing in me and taking a chance on an unproven, "unrecruited" writer despite your "Who's Who" list of Best Selling authors. Like an assistant coach or GM who seeks out unranked players and develops them, you are the best agent in the game. Thanks to Anthony George, the best concierge/assistant in the world, for typing many pages into the twilight hours.

Thanks to Jeff, Robbie, and Michael Feinberg. We began this search for a Coach Wooden story in a Hidden Hills weight room, where your commitment to success and Coach Wooden's Principles inspired me. Jeff, your facility donation at Sierra Canyon High School gave me a place to train, and dream for years with the best coaches and athletic directors in the country. You are a Hall of Fame family. "Why do you think they call it a workout?" ~ Robbie Feinberg.

Thank you to Sierra Canyon Athletic Director David Sobel. Your support of this coach/writer's journey has empowered me, as well as every coach at S.C. You are an All-Star A.D.

Thanks to coaches Bill Self and Rob Judson, who taught me about the power of the bench and the strength of teamwork on an Elite 8 team at Illinois, along with the power of prayer every day at practice. Those lessons led me to place this strong, prayerful team around this project.

Thanks to former NU greats Craig Robinson (and your book "A Game of Character") and Gary Barnett (and your book "High Hopes:

Taking the Purple to Pasadena"), both of which led me to believe in the power of writing. Thanks to Larry Lilja for giving me the shot at NU. Thanks to NU's second winningest coach Bill Carmody for taking a strength coach on the road. Thanks to former NU assistant coach Mitch Henderson for showing me how to overcome the odds by "making shots" while leading Princeton to success.

Thank you to the Day One's for inspiring me to believe, by leaping over high hurdles, and reaching your dreams! Derek Glasser, James Harden, Malik Story, Petey Kass, Jesse Kass, Jason Deutchman, Will Freedman, and Coach Roy White.

Thanks to John, Lynn, Jane, and Charlotte Wirtz for the prayers. Lynn, thanks for bringing me to Willow Creek Church to hear the faith players of the Chicago Bears speak, which inspired my life. Might readers find in John's story what Mike Singletary taught me that night. Thank you for, "Be a dreamer, a star gazer, a rainbow chaser." I chased that rainbow right to this story.

Thank you to the management and staff at Café Gratitude, Bettola, and Vernetti on Larchmont Blvd. below that miraculous double rainbow. Your unending kindness and magic inspired me to keep writing.

Thank you to all the families, athletes and coaches, who supported and inspired me in this journey, by jumping high obstacles.

Thank you to that little fighter Erin, who makes me believe in faith through prayer.

Ultimately, thank you to our God, Who painted Erin's double rainbow and mine, parallel together in the sky, to remind me of His faithfulness.

I love you all!

"The most important thing in the world is family and love."
~ Coach John Wooden.

RAINBOW FOR ERIN

Dribble for Victory Over Cancer combines the efforts of the Pediatric Cancer Research Foundation (PCRF) and the V. Foundation for Cancer Research to combat childhood cancer. This movement builds on the community engagement efforts introduced by the PCRF, UCLA, and St. John's University. Ahead of the season, participating college basketball teams like UCLA, Duke, UNC, etc host events on campus early in the fall. Participants dribble through short on-campus routes to raise funds and awareness for pediatric cancer research. The events allow individuals, families, clubs, and teams to connect with the basketball community, all while contributing to a brighter future for kids and families battling cancer.

A Portion of Proceeds Benefit the Pediatric Cancer Research Foundation

Donate now at pcrf-kids.org

powering cures, realizing futures

Every Cancer Hospital
Every Cancer Patient
Every Cancer Family

Sharing
Hope

PEDIATRIC
CANCER
RESEARCH
FOUNDATION

PUBLISHING STORIES OF
GLOBAL IMPACT
TO THE NATIONS

PUBLISHING · TRANSLATION · DISTRIBUTION

SpiritMedia.US

Made in the USA
Columbia, SC
24 September 2024

42958150R00128